MW00462157

Provoking Your Brilliance!

Provoking Your Brilliance!

Remembering Your Inner Wisdom and Moving from Confusion to Clarity

Machen MacDonald

Provoking Your Brilliance!

Remembering Your Inner Wisdom and Moving from Confusion to Clarity

Machen MacDonald

Published by ProBrilliance
12114 Polaris Drive
Grass Valley, CA 95949
www.ProBrilliance.com

ISBN 0-9764963-0-5

Book design by Peri Poloni, Knockout Design,
Placerville, California
www.knockoutbooks.com

Printed in the United States of America

Contents

Praise for

Provoking Your Brilliance!

"If you're ready to breakthrough to your brilliance – Read this book."

— **MARK VICTOR HANSEN**, Co-Creator, #1 *New York Times* best selling series *Chicken Soup for the Soul®* Co-Author, *The One Minute Millionaire*

"This exciting book shows you how to tap into the unlimited power of your mind and imagination..."

— **BRIAN TRACY**, Author, *Turbo Coach/Goals!*

"More than doubled my income with the information contained in this book. Provoking Your Brilliance! *will "jump start" your self-awareness and self-esteem and put you on the fast track to success. This book introduces the concepts you need to understand who you are and what you really want out of life."*

— **DEBRA J. SATTERWHITE**, Real Estate Consultant

"Provoking Your Brilliance! *is brilliant! Machen MacDonald shows you how to get crystal clear on what you really want in life. Machen also gives you a powerful process you can use right now to turn your ultimate vision into reality."*

— **ROBERT STUBERG**, Founder & Chairman Success.com

"Reading Provoking Your Brilliance! *truly helps you understand why you do the things you do and provides simple yet powerful strategies of how to affect the change you desire."*

— **KENT M. CAMPBELL**, Senior Vice President of Sales AmerUs Life

"In Provoking You Brilliance! *Machen has gathered the threads of his lifetime of learning, leading, and producing results to weave a garment of wisdom. Read this book and wear the wisdom so you can live brilliantly on-purpose."*

— KEVIN W. McCARTHY,
Author, *The On-Purpose Person* and *The On-Purpose Business*

"In a nutshell, it's an excellent "How To..." book for experiencing a fulfilling life."

—CONK BUCKLEY, JR., CLU, ChFC, FLMI,
Regional Sales Director (Retired) AIG/ American General

"Machen's ability to articulate powerful concepts and strategies into simple and easy exercises to affect permanent change is compelling!"

—JAMIE KERCHNER, President Diversified Group

"Machen MacDonald reminds us so eloquently through his ideas and stories how living in "the now" is the very best place to be. If you are ready for self-discovery, the teacher has appeared and his lessons are rich with value."

— JEFF HUGHES,
Financial Services Leadership Development Professional

"When a self made millionaire shares his insights, Listen UP!!! Machen has packed years of strategies, insights and lessons into this book that can support anyone in creating a Happy Healthy Wealthy life."

— JIM BUNCH, Founder of The Happy Healthy Wealthy Game

"Machen MacDonald understands the secrets of attracting success, wealth, and happiness. Let him guide you on the path toward attracting all that you desire to have in your life."

— STACEY HALL AND JAN STRINGER,
Authors, *Attracting Perfect Customers.....The Power of Strategic Synchronicity*

Acknowledgements

I would like to express my deepest love and gratitude to these people that have impacted my life in such an empowering way and from whom I have gleaned great strength, wisdom and love. For without them this book would have no form.

To my wife **Laura** for revealing to me what love, strength, beauty and inner wisdom really are. I love you with all of my being.

To my mom **Shearl** for your unique and loving way of allowing me to find my own way. For making it possible to say I grew up at Lake Tahoe.

To **Marsha and Jules Radow** for allowing me the honor of being part of your family and keeping me on track while allowing great latitude.

To **Seth Radow** for your ongoing brotherly love and support. You are an inspiration.

To my **Nonnie and Grandad** for instilling in me the values and love that guides me. I know you are looking down on me every day.

To all of **my clients** for allowing me the gift of witnessing the brilliance of love and coaching.

To my first coach **Jeanna Gabellini** for introducing me to the world and power of coaching.

To my coach **Jim Bunch** for provoking my brilliance and allowing me the grace to tap my inner wisdom.

To my coach and book shepherd **Robert Stuberg** for your guidance and persistence in bringing this book to life so we can serve others.

To **Julie Pierce** for your excellent editing skills and assemblage of my many thoughts and ideas.

To **Kent Campbell** for always believing in me and my capabilities in the business world and for your ongoing love and support.

To **Diane Ruebling** for demonstrating and teaching me what true visionary leadership is all about. Your love and lessons show up every day.

To **Jeanette Angell, Stan and Eileen Sitko, Jan Rosen, Cindy Campbell, Rick and Deb Satterwhite** Your ongoing love and encouragement are so greatly appreciated.

To **Bob and Emily Collins** for your beautiful example of what a loving, devoted and inspiring relationship can be.

And finally to my children, **Drake, Shane and Adrian** for constantly reminding me of what life and love are truly about. Every father should be blessed and know love as I do from you.

Preface

How to Get the Most Out of This Book

"You can't start a Ferrari with the keys to your first car; you need the right set of keys."

— MACHEN MACDONALD

This book is your guide, your companion, and your toolbox. Just as you benefit from a map to navigate unfamiliar terrain, this book provides you with the topography of undiscovered areas or forgotten treasures within you. Just as a companion joins you on the journey, this book will be with you along the way. Just as the right tool makes a task easier and your efforts more efficient, this book will serve you to that end as well.

As human beings, one of our strongest needs is simply to feel that we are understood. Being understood gives us a sense of control. The stories and examples in this book will confirm that the personal thoughts and feelings you experience every day are experienced by most of us, and how we all struggle with doubt and endeavor to regain control. You are more understood by others than they would lead you to believe and more than you allow yourself to believe. The doubt you experience is a reflection of the uncertainty others have about their own lives. Receive comfort, energy, and confidence from knowing that you and your life matter very much. Your next breath must not be discounted in any way. Embrace it and be grateful, as it may be your last. I say this not to scare or disturb you. I say this to lift you to a higher perspective where you can remember what is really important to you. Only you can decide what is really important for you and your life. Upon picking up this book you may not have made that decision yet. However, by the time you finish this book, I believe you will have the answers you are seeking.

Throughout the book you will see questions, challenges, and exercises. Some are followed by a space for you to write in your answer. To get the most out of this journey, play full-on and engage these investigations as you encounter them. Think, but don't ***over think.*** Your answers don't have to pass any judgments. Nobody but you will see your responses, so be true to yourself. Give yourself permission to capture what is authentically you. You will be glad you did.

It is fascinating that millions of people spend money on audio tapes and books, but only 30% (three out of ten) ever end up reading the books or listening to the audio programs. Of those that do get through the books or programs, an even smaller percentage actually implement what they have learned and affect change in their lives. Most people won't get through the book. My challenge to you is don't be like most people. Commit not only to completing the book, but to actually revisiting it in three months. It's easy enough to do. Simply mark it in your calendar; make an appointment with yourself to reread the book three months from the date you complete it the first time.

As you read through this book you will be provoked to think of your life experience in a new way. Capture those thoughts. Write them down within this book. Mark it up. Dog ear it. Stick notes to it. Then do something magical! Reread the book three months after you have finished it the first time. Check the box to seal your commitment. I commit to reread this book three months after I first complete it. ☐ Date: ___________________

I don't suggest you reread it page by page, unless of course you want to. What I do suggest is that you reengage the wisdom that is presented in the book, including the personal observations you made the first time through. Examine the perspectives and insights that you noted during the first reading, and see how they have shifted compared with your perspectives and insights during follow-up readings.

Why am I challenging you to do this and why should you fully commit to it? Have you ever watched a movie more than once and noticed something different the second time you watched it? Of course! Why was that? Your awareness is at a different level during a subsequent viewing; you are tuning in differently. This is a simple explanation and yet it's a powerful observation. Your awareness and perspectives have changed. In this book you will learn the power of having a preferred perspective.

Many of the included messages and insights are timeless. I didn't make them up. I simply observed, recognized, or discovered what was working for me in my life and the lives of others. Success and happiness leave clues! As you take the principles from this book and apply them in your life, you will inevitably proceed down paths of reality that you may have otherwise not encountered. Ten years from now we will be the same person we are today with the exception of the books we have read and the people we have met. By reading this book you will redirect your path—perhaps only a little bit, but a bit none the less—toward becoming that new person in ten years. This change starts with the person you desire to be today.

I am both honored and excited to be a part of your journey. I look forward to hearing from you and learning about how you are living your brilliance.

Namaste,

Machen

Chapter 1

From Wonder to Wisdom

"It's what you learn after you know it all
that really counts."
— JOHN WOODEN

Before we get started I would like to provide a bit of background about how we as humans tend to process information and learn. One of my primary intentions for this book is to provide you with thought provoking scenarios that will stimulate your inner learning and will serve you in living the life that you have imagined for yourself.

Once you are aware that there are different learning styles as well as clear and distinct learning stages, and once you identify where you are in that process, great and rapid breakthroughs can take place. What follows are explanations and models that will enable you to learn faster, help you embrace the learning process, and move you more quickly towards greater awareness and understanding.

Four Learning Styles

There are many theories about learning styles. The one we look at here is the result of a study done by Peter Honey and Alan Mumford. While each description is an effective instrument for identifying learning stimuli and styles, avoid "labeling" yourself and others. The categorization of each style is merely a convenient simplification of characterizing the differences in learning preferences.

Activist

Activists are people who thrive on immediate experiences. These are usually the first to step forward when a request for volunteers is made. They love activities such as brainstorming. They are gregarious, "ready, fire, aim" people who act first and consider the consequences later. They love to try new things and are bored by routines.

Reflector

Reflectors learn better if they are allowed to sit back and observe. They like to collect information and postpone conclusions. They are cautious and thoughtful and tend to become flustered and frustrated by having to participate in many activities at once.

Theorist

Theorists are logical thinkers and typical perfectionists. They like to adapt and integrate information. They tend to create complex but sound theories. They take information and adapt it to their needs.

Pragmatist

Pragmatists are the experimenters who like to act quickly and confidently to implement new ideas. These are people who feel there must be a better way. They are good at problem solving and tend to be impatient. These individuals come back from meetings and want to institute sweeping changes.

All experimental learning follows the cycle:

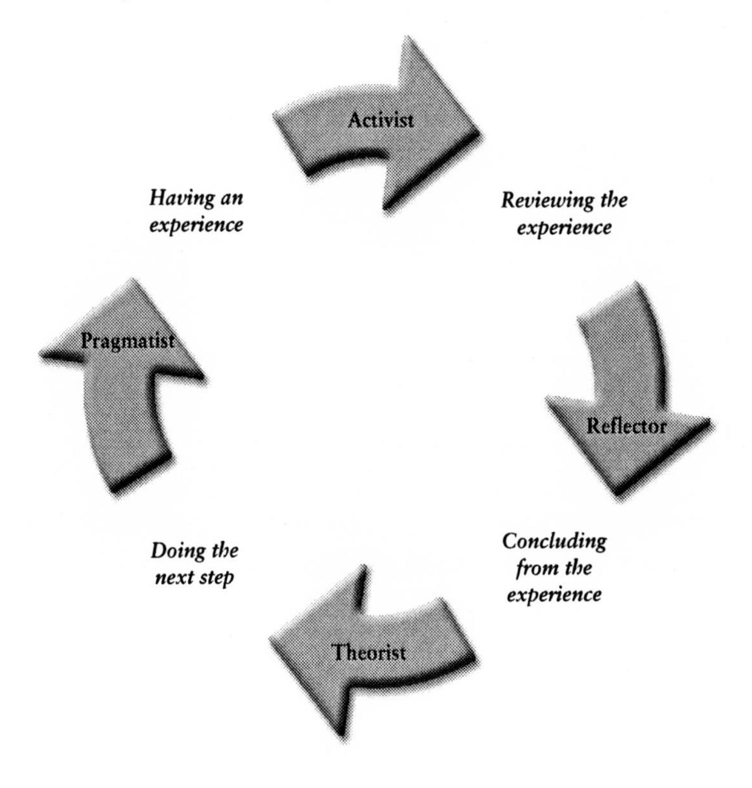

Figure 1 Learning Cycle and Styles

The most significant distinction among the various learning styles is that each one enters the cycle at a different point.

Here is an example to which you can probably relate. My

wife and I recently bought a digital video camera. As soon as we got it home I ripped open the box, discarded the packaging and instructions. I promptly fitted the plugs and adapters into the camera, and attempted to make my first digital motion picture. While I was flailing all over the place, hitting buttons and causing unwanted effects, my wife was patiently reading the directions. She watched me as I cursed, became frustrated, and finally concluded that we bought the wrong camera because I was not getting the desired results. Can you guess my learning style yet? I am as pragmatic as they come.

My wife, on the other hand, expresses more of a theorist style. Right when I was ready to either chuck the new camera through the window or pack it up and take it back to the store, my wife calmed me down and started applying the information she learned from reading the manual. I watched her calmly achieve her desired results. When it was my turn again, I quickly tried to model what she was doing.

That's how I learn. I need to jump in the pool and try to swim, preferably after watching someone else do it. I can play with it and figure it out. My wife is one to read the books and sit through the lectures, get a sufficient amount of data and then apply it. Both styles work. Hers for her and mine for me. Now, if you asked me to read the manual first and then work the equipment, I would be so disconnected that it would probably take me ten times as long to learn something. It's the opposite for my wife. She needs the reference material to study. Otherwise she would be lost and overwhelmed.

For me, what is so liberating about understanding the various learning styles is that I can give myself permission to do it my way and not read the manuals or text books before I get started with a project. If I jump into something and reach a sticking point, then I reference the instructions or seek clarity from some other resource. Identifying your dominant learning style will free you from feeling that you have to learn in a certain way. Each of us is made up of all four styles. However, usually one style is dominant. Our best learning occurs when we are in the part of the learning cycle that matches our dominant learning style.

For many people who are pragmatic or active learners, they learn best by doing versus reading or studying. I see it all the time when I am facilitating various workshops and seminars. If what I am presenting is not applicable or appealing to some of the people at that particular time, then it doesn't provoke the emotion needed to cement the leaning for them. They may be able to regurgitate the information to pass the exam. However, they don't have the burning learning in their being.

By contrast, if what I am presenting immediately impacts their lives, these people are tuned in and engaged in the learning process. It's how you choose to look at it. Are you standing outside the picture, looking at yourself in the picture, or are you looking at your experience from within the picture? You'll get more from yourself if you can be in the picture rather than just seeing yourself in the picture.

A question you can ask yourself that puts you in the picture and in the experience for the best learning is, "Who am I becoming?"

Four Learning Stages

Along with four leaning styles, there are four learning stages. First we must understand the two ingredients needed to help us move through the four stages. Learning is a process that travels from wonder to wisdom. Along the way we experience frustration in varying degrees. Frustration is one of two essential ingredients of learning. The other is curiosity. The trick is to set up your rules so that you can extract the "f," the "u," and the "n" from "frustration" to experience "fun." The figure below illustrates the sequence of the learning stages. Start at the bottom left and work up to the top right.

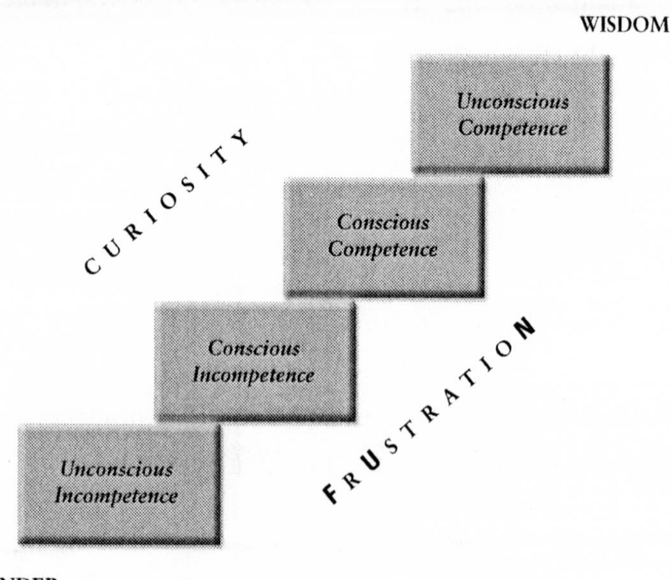

The task at hand determines how long it takes us to move from stage to stage. For some situations it is a matter of minutes, perhaps even seconds, depending on the transferable skills that we bring to the situation. There are some tasks that take years or even a lifetime to master.

In Stage 1, Unconscious Incompetence, you are not yet aware

that you don't know something or don't know how to do something. In Stage 2, Conscious Incompetence, you are aware that you don't know something or don't know how to do something. This is usually where curiosity and frustration begin to dawn. In Stage 3, Conscious Competence, you know something or know how to do something and it takes all of your focus and conscious effort to accomplish the task. In Stage 4, Unconscious Competence, you are aware you know something or how to do something, and it's automatic—you don't even have to think about it.

Can you stand to experience the two essential ingredients needed to learn? Can you deal with having curiosity and frustration surface in your life? Are you one of those people that will do just about anything to avoid these feelings?

You might consider that curiosity is not so bad; you can deal with being or feeling curious. Well, I am talking genuine curiosity. Like Inspector Colombo curiosity. If you are not comfortable with feeling like you don't have all the answers, are not prepared, or are simply stupid, then you have probably done a pretty good job of shutting down your curiosity. The gradual squelching of your curiosity probably happened between the ages of three and seven. Hang out with a four-year-old and count how many times they ask the question "why?" in one day. It will amaze and mentally fatigue you. It may even force you to think. Unfortunately, many youngsters get the message from the adults in their lives that they should stop asking "why?" all the time.

We learn more—expanding our capacity to think and our ability to conceptualize—during the first seven years of our lives, than we do for the entire remainder of our existence. One theory states that in losing our genuine curiosity, we also lose the ability to become skillfully inquisitive. If you have children please, please, please encourage them to ask questions. You might even learn something yourself. I have learned a ton by looking at life through the eyes of my children.

Questions indicate the presence of the first essential ingredient, curiosity. Don't be so impatient to jump to the answer. Force them and yourself to think; come to your own conclusions. It is about engaging the power to think. Help your children and yourself develop reasoning and critical thinking skills. Encourage experimentation; it's okay to get it wrong. You'll figure out when the "right" answer needs to be revealed. It really is a matter of having faith and trusting that the answer will reveal itself when it is time.

When you insist that your child figure out the answer to the question, you will inevitably witness the second ingredient needed for learning. This usually occurs right before the smoke starts coming out of their ears. This type of scenario indicates the presence of the second essential ingredient, frustration. Think back to when you were thoroughly frustrated and you kept going. Wasn't that the point when your breakthrough, awaking or shift occurred? It was in that moment that you got it. The light bulb turned on.

For some of us, as soon as we experience the frustration, we are wired to give up and not ask that one more question or give it one more attempt. We just automatically shut down. For others, we realize that directly following the experience of frustration, the answer is revealed. If we just keep going, the breakthrough occurs. This is transformational learning. When we get that Aha! then learning has occurred at the deepest level. We will not forget it like we did 99% of the memorized material on our school exams.

There are plenty of football teams that can march down the field ninety-nine yards and fail to get over the goal line, and it is not uncommon to see the losing team have more yardage than the team that won. The difference is the winning team managed to move the ball across the goal line. In our scenario, the goal line is the learning point or the breakthrough to understanding. And the great thing about life—unlike football—is you get as many chances as you want, and eventually you will cross the goal line. You get to keep going until you experience your breakthrough; regardless of the time left on the clock or the number of attempts. The number of attempts is not the issue. Each attempt adds an awareness that is necessary to eventually experience the learning. Embrace the attempts along the way to your wisdom.

In the four stages of learning or mastery, it is Stage 4 that you must aspire to. John Wooden, the great UCLA basketball coach often said, "It's what you learn after you know it all that really counts." This is the first step of the next paradigm via your new awareness.

Some examples will help you understand the four stages even better. Unconscious Incompetence is not knowing where your nose is on your face. Can you recall back that far? Another example is not being aware that you don't know how to drive a car.

Let's explore the first example: One day you become aware you have this thing on your face with two holes and that your fingers are perfectly sized for insertion. You still are not sure what it is. All you know in your fresh little brain is that you don't know. You are aware of something new that requires further exploration. Meanwhile Mommy and Daddy are asking you where this two-holed object is with the repetitive expression of "ware-shor-noze," which you later interpret to mean "where's your nose." While they are posing this question, they are also pointing to the two-holed objects on their own faces and then touching yours. You are quite clear about the fact that you do not know what they are trying to tell you. You have become Consciously Incompetent and are in Stage 2.

In your grand wisdom you wrinkle a frown of perplexed concern, and Mommy and Daddy try even harder to get their point across. You begin to make the connection. But before you get this mastered, they and all the relatives start bombarding you with the mid-term for Anatomy 101. You become overwhelmed and frustrated by the questions and something clicks. You suddenly get it!

Emerging from this confusion and commotion, you realize your nose is that center point on your face. Ta Da! You are now Consciously Competent and in Stage 3. You now know the sound "noze" refers to that thing in the middle of your face. Now you tie in some motor-skills, and when Mommy and Daddy ask "ware-shor-noze," you promptly flail your chubby little arm with chubby digits attached and smack yourself on the nose.

Eventually after practicing this exercise repeatedly, you don't really need to think it through anymore. You are now Unconsciously Competent, achieving Stage 4. You went through the four stages of learning while moving from curiosity to frustration to understanding.

Curiosity was there. Mommy and Daddy had your attention, you were trying desperately to help them through their agitation, and you were curious to understand what would put them at ease. You became aware of that something on your face is known as your nose. However, at the time you didn't know what it was and yet you were curious. Then you experienced frustration. Your parents' persistence and the introduction of the mid-term exam by the extended family overwhelmed you, and you traveled through the four stages of learning. Here is the really important part: Mommy and Daddy probably made it a game of some kind. They made it fun. So think of ways to make learning fun for yourself.

When I am confused or frustrated, I celebrate because my brain is searching for an answer and I am about to learn something new. This belief is fun and exciting! You'll agree that it's a lot better than, "I just don't get it. It's too complicated. Why bother?" It's all about which approach you choose to take. Choose wisely.

Refer again to Figure 1 Wonder to Wisdom, and notice that Stage 2 and Stage 3 are in the frustration zone. By the way zone is noze spelled inside out. Just having a little fun! Perhaps it will help you recall the connection between the story of learning about your noze and the importance of the frustration zone. So next time you are feeling overwhelmed or frustrated with a situation rejoice. You are right where you are supposed to be. You are on the cusp of a major breakthrough. Keep trying! You get all the tries you want.

I have come to realize that if I don't have a feeling of frustration several times a day, I am not learning anything. What's the value in that? And speaking of values, can you tell that learning is one of mine? You can bet that I have set up my work and home life in a way that allows me to honor this value every day.

In fact, I have structured my career to get paid for learning things of interest to me. Once I've got it, I abridge the information and teach others what I have learned.

It took a lot of conditioning for me to get comfortable with frustration and to become skilled at reframing frustration as a good and empowering feeling. I still have to work at it. It seems I am only Consciously Competent at it. I am getting there. You can too. It won't happen over night so hang in there. Or, who knows, it may be easier for you.

I specifically chose the word "conditioning" in the previous paragraph. Reworking the way you perceive, look at, or feel about things takes conditioning. It's like getting a muscle into shape. If you haven't stepped into a gym in a while, you don't just decide to get into physical shape, hit the gym once, and PA-BAHM you're in shape. It takes a lot of sessions at the gym with focused, intense effort to knock off those extra pounds and firm up those flabby muscles.

Getting your thinking into the shape you want takes some work too. But just as you look in the mirror and become aware you have some bulges and curves in the wrong places, you may also need to reflect on your thinking. The best mirror is the quality of your life. If your life is not exactly what you want it to be, then your thinking needs some re-conditioning.

Chapter 2

Already a Perfect 10

"Strive to affect others profoundly."
— THOMAS LEONARD

At the beginning of my seminars and workshops I often start by holding up a $10 bill and asking the question, "Who would like this $10 bill?" Hands shoot into the air.

"I am going to give this to one of you, but first let me do this." Then I crumple up the bill.

"Who wants it now?" Still, the hands are up in the air.

"Well, what if I do this?" I shout some demoralizing comments at the bill, dropping it on the ground, and grinding it into the floor with my shoe.

I pick it up, the now crumpled and dirty bill. "Now who wants it?" Still, hands are in the air.

"My friends, you have all learned a very valuable lesson. No matter what I do to this money, you still want it; it does not decrease in value. It is still worth $10."

Many times in our lives, we are screamed at, dropped, crumpled, and ground into the dirt by the decisions we make and the way we process the experiences that come our way. We feel that we are worthless (worth less). But, no matter what has happened or what will happen, you never lose your value. Dirty or clean, crumpled or finely pressed, you are sill priceless to those who love you. And you should be one of those that love you the most. The worth of our lives comes not in what we do, or whom we know, but in who we are. You are special.

Try this:

1. Name the five wealthiest people in the world.
2. Name the last five Heisman trophy winners.
3. Name the last five winners of the Miss America contest.
4. Name ten people who have won the Nobel or Pulitzer Prize.
5. Name the last half dozen Academy Award winners for best actor and actress.
6. Name the last decade's worth of World Series winners.

How did you do?

Most of us eventually forget the headliners of yesterday. The people whose names answer the quiz are no second-raters. They are the best in their fields. But the applause dies. Awards tarnish. Achievements are forgotten.

Here's another quiz. First rank yourself emotionally at this moment on a scale of 1 to 10. 1 means you feel like a crumpled up dejected $10 bill and have all but given up on living life, and

10 means you are a fresh crisp $10 bill ready for circulation; you are really feeling fantastic about yourself and your life. Circle the number that best describes your current state of being at this moment:

1 2 3 4 5 6 7 8 9 10

Read the following list and as you do, write down the names of the people that come to mind:

1. List a few teachers who aided your journey through school.

___

___

___

2. Name three friends who have helped you through a difficult time.

___

___

___

3. List six people who have taught you something worthwhile. What did they teach you?

___

___

___

4. Think of a few people who have made you feel appreciated and special. What did they do and how did you process it?

___

___

___

___

5. Think of six people you enjoy spending time with.

____

____

____

6. Name half a dozen heroes whose stories have inspired you.

____

____

____

Was this quiz much easier?

Now that you have listed these special people and have mentally and emotionally revisited some of the special situations in your life, rank how you are feeling—your state of being—at this moment as a result of doing this exercise. Circle the number that best describes your current state of being at this moment:

1 2 3 4 5 6 7 8 9 10

Did you move up the scale? Conclusion: The people who make a difference in your life are not the ones with the most credentials, the most money, or the most awards. They are the ones that care.

First and foremost you are the number one person in your life. You must care about yourself; you must love yourself. You don't have to be a statistic from the first quiz to matter or be revered by people. However, you should strive to show up on the second quiz as much as possible not only for yourself but for as many people as you can—especially for those that you care about. Strive to affect yourself and others profoundly. Remember, you may be just one person in the world and to one person you may be the world.

Chapter 3

The Grass Is Greener Where You Water It

"We cannot teach people anything; we can only help them discover it within themselves."
— GALILEO GALILEI

No matter how bad you think your situation is at this moment there is always someone else whose life is more screwed up than yours. This may or may not be comforting for you to know. However, think about this for a moment: If you had the opportunity to put all your troubles or problems—or shall we call them challenges—into a hat, and everybody else you know did the same with their own hats, is there anybody in the world you would really trade hats with knowing you could never get your own hat back?

I am positive if you really consider the situations, both theirs and yours, you would not trade, not even if only for one day. I don't care how good somebody looks on the outside—whether it's his or her physical appearance, their grand home, their occupational status, their social status, their fame and fortune or their health. If you lived just one day in their life as them experiencing their desires and accomplishments as well all the roller coaster of emotions that go with each, it would be so foreign to you that you would be screaming to wake up from the nightmare.

There is something to be said for familiarity. Actually a lot can be said. So what does familiarity mean to you? What does feeling familiar give you? Ask yourself, does it provide comfort? Does it allow you predictability? Does familiarity mean some kind of sense of security? Whatever it is to you, it is...for now anyway.

Your greatest gift is your ability to choose and choose again. It's also called free will!

It's your choice. What WILL you choose?

____

What's the choice you have not been making that you know you must?

____

____

You may have heard people say, "You are right where you are supposed to be in life," or "It is God's will," or one of my favorites, "You create your own reality." Well, I am here to tell you they are all true! The fact is you have a choice. The greatest gift you are blessed with is your own free will. Your ability to think and make decisions for yourself is one of the keys that we will discover together through the course of this book. Along with the opportunity to make your own choice and the prospect to act on it comes the consequence of those actions.

Now hold on, I am still on your side. I struggled and I mean s-t-r-u-g-g-l-e-d with these oh so comforting phrases for thirty-nine years of my life. I wanted to believe them. After all, they are pretty comforting. They give us permission to not beat ourselves up for all the less-than-perfect endeavors that make up the mosaic of a life thus far. They just seemed to make it too easy. Well, that's what I used to think. Remember, I was all about struggle. After all, if something was worth having, it was worth working hard for. And somewhere along the way, I translated hard work into struggle.

Even though I had been exposed to what I now know are the solutions to much of the struggle I encountered or created, I continued to struggle. It felt like I was driving forward while blind folded, directed by my "gremlin" giving me instructions based on what he saw in the rearview mirror. I haven't introduced you to my gremlin yet, have I? Have you been introduced to yours? The gremlin can show up as what seems a mindless defeatist voice that drills into you and reminds you of things that are not the most up-lifting or empowering. It may say things like, "you're not good enough" or "don't go for it, you'll just screw it up and embarrass us all." Sometimes they ask, "Who are you to think you deserve that much money or get that promotion?" I am sure you've heard the voice. As Rick Carson explains in his book Taming Your Gremlin© 1983 Richard D. Carson—your gremlin is the "narrator" in your head. Gremlin Taming® is a specific method developed by Rick Carson and described in his seminal work Taming Your Gremlin®. I would encourage you to explore his method further as what follows is a reflection of my own experience and not an in depth explanation of Carson's approach.

You may know this voice by another name such as the inner critic, mind monster, or perhaps you have named it something like Loud Loser Lester.

Here's the shocker! It may even be the words, phrases, or mantras expressed in the loving voice of someone who cares for us very much. It may be our dear grandmother's voice who, when we want something, says in a very endearing voice in our head now, "Oh honey, you don't need to have that." That was just Grandma's way of protecting us from the heartache that nobody could afford it at the time. Or maybe you wanted to do something that would take time away from your relationship with her. Or maybe she didn't really understand what it was, and because she had no need for it, why should anybody else? It could be a hundred and one reasons why she was afraid to let it into her experience. However, all we know is that she loved us very much, took good care of us, and must have known something we didn't, especially since we were only five years old. We are not five any more. How many things, relationships, and opportunities have you backed down from to make the voice right? Were you even aware that's what you were doing to yourself? Are you still doing it? What's your plan to break that cycle? Use this model to assist you in breaking the cycle of the limiting chant that holds you back.

On an index card or on a blank piece of paper write the words Awareness in Action. Number it 1 through 6 on the left side. Throughout your day notice and become aware of the limiting mantras that surface within you. In addition to noticing the negative chant, identify where it came from. Whose voice is it? How did you adopt it? Find the gift in it. How did the mantra serve you? Commit to deleting the limiting mantra and create a more empowering script. Here is an easy example. "Don't talk to strangers." Parents dropped this one in. It served me by not becoming involved in what may have become dangerous situations. I am now an adult and it doesn't serve me, so I may delete it. My new mantra is, "Strangers are just friends and advocates I have not met yet, and I am pleasing to myself in the presence of others. I introduce myself first."

Struggle literally vanished once I dealt with the mind monster and squelched the voice that repeatedly insisted struggle was noble, or persuaded me against something with, "Oh, honey, you don't need that!" Also, once I redefined what struggle meant to me, I knew true freedom. I had created a jail sentence in my own mind. It's not the bars that keep the tiger in the cage; it is the space between the bars.

My old definition of struggle was that if things didn't go perfectly the first time I would keep trying pretty much the same way, hoping that the results would change. That's also the definition of insanity. So, I formed a new definition for myself. It goes like this: I can only struggle if, after I try varied approaches that may not get the intended results, I have not made any progress, and I have not learned something new. With a new rule set up this way, it's hard to struggle. Persistence and tenacity are great and admirable qualities. Please don't confuse them with struggle as I did in the past.

In what areas of your life is there struggle?________________

What is your current rule about struggle? ________________

____

____

____

How does struggle serve you? ________________________

____

____

____

What does struggle give you? ___________________________

____

____

____

What does struggle protect you from having to do that you know you must? ____

____

____

____

I know the more empowering truths to be self-evident. "You are right where you are supposed to be" is true. How can you be anywhere else? Only your mind can trick you into thinking you can be somewhere else. The real power comes in lining up your mind here now with your body here now. It is like aligning the tumblers of a lock—when they are lined up, things just open right up.

"It is God's will" can be a tough one to accept especially with all the perceived tragedies and negative, mindless events that fill the newspapers and news shows. Remember this—God gave us free will, the ability to think for ourselves. He also gave us the power and strength to overcome anything that may happen during our lifetime. 99.9% of that power is our ability to choose what we allow our minds to focus on. Our minds can only focus on one thing at a time. In the chaos of the thousand thoughts whirling around in our heads at any one time, the mind can only focus on one of them at a time. The juke box can only play one record at a time. Those people that you may see as having courage, strength of mind, and their act together have simply mastered their ability to focus on what is positive and empowering within a given situation. It's all in how you look at things. Your glass is either half full or half empty. You decide! I will tell you this, I am grateful to just have the glass. Are you? The glass is life. If you don't like what's in it, pour it out and go fill it with what you desire for yourself!

The one I really wanted to believe because it sounded so magical as if I could just snap my fingers and instantly manifest whatever I wanted is: "You create your own reality." As I finally got this one, it has made the world of difference for me and those that I share it with. Initially however I was looking at it from the wrong side. I was looking at it from the outside rather than the inside. Much of this book will be devoted to this idea and how understanding it can give us a sense of control over our lives.

In a nutshell, it is our thoughts that affect our behavior and our behavior effects our actions. Our actions or inactions cause a result. This is cause and effect. It is how the universe works. This cause and effect cycle creates our circumstances. We must take responsibility for our circumstances. If we follow the decision path, we find that our thoughts and actions lead up to what we have and where we are now. How we choose to look at and experience our circumstances is our power—our power to create our reality. Our reality is how we choose to look at or experience our circumstances.

The three truths that we've discussed here have become part of my guiding principles. I now fully know these to be true. Not only do I know them, but I live them. By the time you finish this book, they may be guiding principles for your life too. These are not the only three truths or guiding principles. However, if these three are not among your top ten, that fact may explain why you picked up this book for answers.

During the time I was in struggle mode and doing my best to defy and disprove these truths, it felt like I was spinning my wheels. I was trading my present for my future. Let's examine the word "present" for a moment. It can either mean to be in a specified place; existing or happening now. Or it can mean a gift. My new definition of the word present is the gift of being here now. By accepting this gift, I can, in retrospect, see I was right where I was supposed to be in my life each and every moment. It was God's will, and I was creating my own reality. In the past, my constant experience of struggle was a result of my having strung so many moments together, of not accepting, and of not being aware of the gift. That struggle provided me all that I needed to experience. It brought me to the point of writing this book, which I started at three o'clock in the morning, September 11, 2002—one year after the tragic 9/11 event.

The reality from my perspective is that it took me this long to get it. I read all the books, heard all the speakers, and listened to all the tapes, and it took me thirty-nine years to finally listen to myself. Do you realize the significance of the last statement? Learn to listen to yourself!

There is a Buddhist saying: "When the student is ready the teacher will appear." Remembering this helps me not beat myself up so much when I seem to have taken a while to learn a life lesson. What also helps is realizing that the teacher comes in many forms. One of my intentions is to have this book serve you as one of your teachers. Keep this in mind as you continue on your journey. It is only in life that we are first given the test followed by the lesson. In school we first get the assignment of learning the lesson, and then we are given the test. Are you beginning to sense why you may have some uncertainty in your life and feel like you missed the homework assignment or didn't prepare properly for this thing called life? The sooner you can accept that the test precedes the lesson and be okay with it, the sooner you can move forward into the experience of the joyful and vibrant life that is yours.

Don't sweat the fact that you went this many years without this realization. Just be aware of where you are right now. Are you in lesson mode or test mode? Don't concern yourself with the sequence just be aware. And, often you may not be aware until you have shifted from one to the other and are well into that mode. Is there really even a difference between the two? It's your choice. You decide!

Consult your memory, retain your future, and be in the moment. Life is a sequence of moments. You are either aware you're in the moment or you are not. To be present in the moment is balance. It is where your truth and power are. If you are anywhere else other than your truth, you are surrendering your power.

Here is a little perspective game: What do you see here?

N O W H E R E

Some see the words "now here" and others see "no where." It's the same seven letters; it's just a simple example of how your focus affects your results. Did you focus on the left or the right of the "W"? A small shift can mean a big difference. If you are present, you are Now Here. If you are either focusing on the past or the future you are No Where since the past is over and does not exist except for our recollection, and the future has not happened yet. The past and the future are, in essence, no man's land. To place our focus there is to surrender our power which lies in the present moment. So what is the new perspective from which you want to start living your life?

From this point on, I commit to living my life as much as possible from the perspective of:

____.

Dated:____________________

Signed:________________________________

Learn in one moment what it took me thirty-nine years to figure out. And for me the "it" is that I really do have a choice in the decision to either be happy, to have total peace of mind, or to be unhappy and miserable. You and everybody on this planet have the same choice. The power comes in knowing how to use it. It's all about choice.

Here is a perfect example that occurred while I was writing this book. I have this wonderful computer, however after two and one-half years, 200,000 frequent flyer miles later, and nearly twenty gigs of creation it is a bit temperamental. It suddenly began making an annoying sound. The alarming sound was not one usually associated with a fully functioning laptop, at least not in my experience. It sounded like it was about to go to the great laptop travel case in the sky.

I caught myself starting to curse the blasted machine. And then quickly realized what a great and awesome tool it is and all that it provides me. However, if you heard the sound it was making you would run for cover. My point is that my reaction to the sound was determined by how I chose to look at the situation. How I would experience that moment was my choice.

I could have continued to focus on the noise and curse and berate the beast, getting myself totally off track and out of flow. Or, I could do a 180-degree turn and find the positive in it, which for me is that the laptop enables me to bang out this book quicker than if I had to scratch it out with pad and pencil. The realization that I was confronted with choices is the important point here. I could either continue down the path of trying to confirm that the computer was going to mess with me and provide me with a bunch of trouble and heartache should it crash, or I could follow the path of action to retain what I had created thus far. I could also go down the path of having a brand new computer. It is clear that I had choices as we all do in any given situation. Now, I had to make a decision. That's usually the difficult part.

I am reminded of a story that helps me keep a healthy perspective when things don't appear, on the surface, to be going right. There was a little boy who really wanted a pony. Every day he asked his mom and dad for his own pony. They lived in an apartment complex in the city, so Mom and Dad tried to explain to their son that it was not a good idea to keep a pony in an apartment. Every day for months and months the little boy would make his request. Some days his requests were more spirited than others. Mom and Dad were at their wits end. They felt they were just not getting their son to understand that it was not practical. Then it dawned on them if they could discourage the boy, he might give up asking for the pony. To this end, Dad took drastic measures. He had several loads of horse manure delivered to the apartment. He had it dumped in the boy's room, waiting for him to return home from school. The parents were sure their son would no longer want the pony once he realized the mess it would make and the responsibility it would take to keep and care for a pony.

About three o'clock that afternoon the little boy returned home. When he walked into the apartment he inquired about the new smell that filled the apartment. Mom and Dad looked at each other trying not to smile as they watched their plan unfold. The boy went to his room. Less than a minute later the parents heard the boy screaming. They were now confident that the boy would want nothing to do with having a pony and that their problems were over. However, when they peaked into his room they saw their son playing in the manure, digging away, actually swimming in it while screaming joyfully. The parents looked at each other in complete disbelief. They asked their son if he knew that he was covered in manure. He replied with an ever innocent "Yes," and thanked his Mom and Dad for the pony. The parents were beside themselves. The Dad asked his son, "How can you be so happy with your room full of manure and you covered in it?" The boy, with the biggest smile you ever saw and a spirit so bright, said to his Mom and Dad, "With all this manure, there has got to be a pony in here somewhere?"

How is that for having the right attitude? With that much conviction and determination, how could such spirit not be contagious? I suspect that the three of them found a way for the boy to have a pony. If the conviction is strong enough, the desired outcome will most likely not be denied. Although there may be what seems like a delay in gratification, do not confuse the delay with denial. Maintain the spirit of conviction.

What delay are you mistakenly confusing with denial? Is your conviction strong enough?

For those of you reading and saying, "Okay, but the kid may not have really gotten the pony," let me help you. While he was playing in the manure, he was sure he most certainly had a pony! Think about it. We make up lies that we believe all the time, although they are usually not helpful or supportive. Put your belief in that which is helpful and supportive to your convictions.

So, what is the self-defeating lie you have been living? For me it was that I'm not good enough and my contributions are not important. What's yours?

____

____

____

____

____

____

Chapter 4

Beliefs, Values, and Perfection

"Few are those who see with their own eyes and feel with their own hearts."

— ALBERT EINSTEIN

Every moment of every day you have a choice. You can talk yourself into cracking open a cold one and plopping in front of the TV, or you can tell yourself you are a world-class dad and do something fun with the kids. You can take a nap, or you can envision your future and summon the energy to make progress in what you really want to do with your life. You can hit the snooze alarm for the third time, or you can get up an hour earlier every day and devote that hour to doing that important thing you want to do for which there never seems to be enough time.

You know all of this already, right? I hear you. You're saying,

"Mach, I know what to do, I just can't get myself to do it," or "I don't know how, specifically, to do it." Not to worry, by the time you are done with this book you will know how to get yourself to do what you want to do. The "How" is different for each and every one of us. The "How" is not your concern, although that is where most people will focus their energy as it is the ego's illusion that it should be a concern. The real "How" is revealed in the "Why." There are as many "Whys" as there are people. That's the good news. Stay with me, I am not going to leave you hanging.

In his audio program Getting Things Done Fast, author David Allen explains that there are really only two problems in life. Isn't that great to know, that every single problem anybody has—including you—can ultimately be narrowed down to one of the following two problems:

1. You know what you want and don't know how to get it.

-OR-

2. You don't know what you want.

I love the Nike slogan "Just Do It!" If I know what I am doing I can stop sucking my thumb and "Just Do It." Thank you very much! It implies that you know what you want and you know how to get it. For many of us that is only half the equation. More often, we don't know how to get what we know we want. And, if I have no clue how to proceed, I can't "Just Do It!" I could probably Just Break It! I could Just Screw It Up! I could Just Lose It! But don't tell me "Just Do It!" Please! Here we need to take inventory and asses our skill set. We need to evaluate our level of readiness. We all have varying skill levels. We all have areas in which we excel. Have you discovered yours?

If you become brilliant at only one thing in life let it be this: Controlling your state of mind. You can't control the state of affairs. You can however control your state of mind. Doug Lennick in his book Simple Genius You says it like this, "Happiness is a state of mind...not a state of affairs." That is right on target. Isn't that what we are really in search of? Aren't we all ultimately looking to feel happy? Don't we all seek peace of mind? When you are asked, "What do you want for your children?" don't you usually respond with, "I just want them to be happy"? Isn't that what we really want for ourselves too? There is so much out there that is beyond our immediate control or even our influence. However, the one thing that we do have total control over—though it may not seem like it some or even most of the time—is our state of mind, our current thoughts and what we focus on.

We may not be able to consciously direct or control the circumstances in which we find ourselves. We do, however, have the power to focus from a healthy perspective on those circumstances. This philosophy is illustrated by the Bucket Theory. The Bucket Theory says that all problems or situations can be placed into one of three buckets. This is a tool that will help you invest your time and energy focusing on the tasks that you have control over and on which you can have an impact. Often people get trapped spending too much time and energy in areas where they have little impact. Having the Bucket Theory as a part of your life philosophy can help facilitate the rapid identification of whether the issue at hand is something that should take up any of your time or energy.

Bucket #1: You have total control of changing or improving the situation. Direct 85% or more of your time and energy to Bucket # 1 issues.

Bucket #2: You don't have decision-making power or control to change or improve the situation however, you do have the ability to influence the situation or the people that do. Direct only 10%–15% but no more than 20% of your time and energy to issues in Bucket #2.

Bucket #3: You have no control, decision-making power, or influence to change or improve the situation. Thus, you must work within the parameters of the situation. Gravity would be an excellent example of a Bucket # 3 issue. Direct no more than 5% of your time and energy to issues in Bucket # 3. Usually, that 5% will take the form of venting or releasing the energy and frustration that may be experienced with Bucket # 3 issues.

The human mind can only focus on one thing, just one thing at a time. Since that is the case it should seem pretty easy to control just one thing at time. The reality is that it isn't easy unless you train and condition yourself to control your thoughts. Thoughts are things. They are intangible. They are perhaps precursors to tangible things. However, they, themselves are things. Every thing you see, hear, feel or experience in any way began as a thought in your or someone else's mind. This book is a result of my thoughts. The information gathered in these pages comprises some original thoughts and some thoughts from other people. The chair you are sitting in is a result of someone's thought. Before it was built or manufactured, someone envisioned it, saw it in his or her mind's eye; thought it. The car you drive, and the streets and bridges you drive on all started with a thought.

Since thoughts are things in the seed stage it is imperative to provide them with the healthiest of nurturing environments. It is no different than a garden. The challenge for most of us is that we want it to be harvest season all of the time. We tend to forget that there are four seasons, and during each season we must perform differently to accomplish what we ultimately want.

"The greatest achievement was at first and for a time (only) a dream."

— JAMES ALLEN

I recently moved out of the suburbs to a rural area in northern California. We have five acres and the home of our dreams, which, by the way, at one point in my life was only a thought. Ten years ago when I was living in an 800-square-foot, one-bedroom apartment with my new bride, I started creating the vision, the thought of what I really wanted for myself and my family. At the time, I didn't have this crystal clear vision that came down from the heavens and filled my mind, body, and soul with what I wanted. All I knew was that I wanted more space—at least one more room. Well, be careful what you ask for or think. You often times get it.

Our first home that we bought, after renting the apartment, was a two-bedroom home. That's right, at least one more room than we previously had. The new home was great…for a while. Then we started having children, who, I am convinced, are magnets for all that is plastic regardless of shape, size, and color. I started working out of the home and all my office stuff took over the dining room. Computers, filing cabinets, phones, books, paper, and more paper. Did I mention paper? Our home reminded me of one of those plastic toys you see in birthday goodie bags. You know the one. It's a flat square and has eleven numbered movable squares inside of twelve spaces. You slide the squares around in the spaces, and the goal is to get them lined up in numerical order. Our two-bedroom home was just like that. We had so much stuff with the two boys, my wife, myself, and my work that if you wanted to go into one room you had to move stuff from one room to another so you could fit into the desired room. I think the technical term is "clutter." And that state was an outside manifestation of my thoughts.

Let's revisit the idea of the garden, which is a great analogy for how your thoughts work. Thoughts are just like seeds. Inside a carrot seed is the essence or universal intent of a carrot. Within a watermelon seed is the essence of watermelon, and so it is for each of the different seeds. If you plant a corn seed it will yield only corn and nothing else. You can't get a tomato from a cucumber seed. What I want to know is who spilled the bag of weed seeds in my garden! Weeds are those negative, pernicious thoughts that scatter blast inside our minds all day like pinballs on uppers. Somehow they just get in, and if we are not careful they can rule and ruin a life.

With each seed that my boys and I planted from the package beautifully illustrated with the picture of the mature vegetable, we envisioned what our garden would be like when all its bounty would flourish. We saw ourselves coming down to the garden to pick lettuce, cucumbers, and tomatoes for a salad. This was great! And so we finished putting the seeds into the ground.

But were we done? Of course we were not done! We have to water each day. Pull weeds. Fertilize. Before even planting any seeds we needed to get the earth ready to accept the seeds. In our case we had a full day of fun wrestling a roto-tiller. At least Dad did anyway. During the first couple of weeks, it appeared that nothing was growing in our garden and perhaps our efforts were wasted. As far as we could tell nothing was breaking though the surface other than a few intrusive weeds. The boys were excited about the weeds thinking they were the beginnings of corn, perhaps a carrot, or maybe even a pumpkin that would be ready in time for Halloween. When I told them these were weeds that we had to pull out, they were reluctant still hoping that these were sprouts of nourishing veggies.

I have noticed that many people, including me, tend to allow the weeds of our mind—the negative thoughts—to take root instead of pulling them out as soon as they show up. Rather, we begin to cultivate them. How crazy is that? Why do we hang on to the weeds and cultivate them as if they are what we want? One answer is because they are familiar to us. Unfortunately, for many of us, our minds practically default to growing weed thoughts. After all, aren't we creatures of habit? Don't we proceed down the path of least resistance? It is a huge challenge to shift out of our comfort zone temporarily to create the life we really want! The trick, and one that we will explore in depth a bit later, is creating new comfort zones. If you think about it, hanging onto old comfort zones is about as crazy as trying to squeeze into the desk you sat at when you were in second grade. You know why they made those desks so small back then? So we would eventually leave and not come back having grown out of them. It's about growing folks. Just like the garden. If you are not growing, you are rotting.

Some of us grow a pretty prolific garden of weeds, and we are proud of it. I did and, boy-howdy, was I proud of that weed garden. I would show it off to anybody that came my way. By the way, I didn't think that I was the one planting and cultivating it. I thought I was just the lucky recipient of the garden. Some people received a garden of lettuce; some a garden of melons; some a garden of mixed veggies, and others a flower garden or perhaps a fruit orchard. That's just the way it was—I thought. And what a trapping thought that was.

So who is responsible for what grows in the garden? Is it the boss? Is it the team? Is it our parents? Is it Ms. Green from the third grade? Or is it the gardener? You guessed it, Farmer Brown! Each of us is responsible for our own garden! Right now you have a choice to make. You can start pulling the weeds out by the roots and make room for your desired harvest—the life you really want—or you can just let the weeds take over. Nobody said it was going to be easy. It's simple and yet it's not easy.

Until you have conditioned yourself and developed the right muscles physically, mentally, and emotionally, it is going to be some work and well worth it. Keep the faith! Often times we get lulled into thinking or feeling that our situation is not that bad. We tell ourselves things like, "I have gotten this far. It's too late to change." We talk ourselves into living the fantasy that life's not that bad, it could be worse, and that fire we once had inside that has been smoldering is just about out. We hallucinate that we have some level of certainty.

The quality of your life is in direct proportion to your ability to handle uncertainty. Don't let the fire within go out! Is it scary? Oh yes, you bet! It's scary for anybody. I don't care who you are. What gets us through it is courage. Courage is feeling the fear, digging down deep, and doing what you know you must do to get to the other side. And there is another side. You know there is! Give yourself whatever permission you need to get there. See yourself living it. Hear it, smell it, feel it!

Just as a farmer needs the right tools and the right environment to ultimately harvest the benefits of his work, you will need the right tools. What are the elements that a gardener must contend with? The quality of the soil and its nutrients; watering and irrigation; the threat of insects, birds, and other animals like deer or raccoons; the weather; selection of the right kind of seeds; proper use of fertilizer.

Growing your mind and harvesting the life you desire is no different really. Your thoughts are the seeds. Be careful which ones you plant and where you plant them. The fence around the garden represents our boundaries, values, and rules we must set up for ourselves to keep the threats out. I have seen people sacrifice their values for the achievement of a goal that isn't even theirs, a goal that they have been sold by their boss, team, parents, or someone else. The threats to our garden are the animals that come to pluck our fruit before we can. They are the negative nay-sayers, the people that tell you to accept your lot in life, that you can't do or become what you want. It can be the colleague that steals the accolades for your job well done. It can be the boss that fears surrounding himself with stronger people that can help him achieve greatness. They may be cleverly disguised as very loving people who want to "protect" you. They preach things like,

"Don't attempt to do that. You'll just be disappointed when it doesn't work out." They really do care. They don't want to see you get hurt. However, what is it costing you to buy into that? What is disappointment anyway? Whose definition have you adopted? Most people set up the rules around disappointment to be something like this: If it doesn't go according to plan, then I will feel bad and pout around to inform everybody that the force wasn't with me on that endeavor.

Would you like to know how to set up a rule about disappointment that would make it almost impossible for you to feel that negative emotion? Here is a new belief that I have adopted; see if it works for you. I can only be disappointed if I've exhausted all possibilities for having things go the way I plan, and only after I've ascertained that nothing positive happened as a result of the situation. Do you think I feel disappointment too often anymore? To be honest with you, since I have adopted this new belief around disappointment I don't experience it anymore. Do I feel it coming on sometimes? Sure. Do I now have a new tool to pull the weed out before it even takes root? Absolutely!

Where do we get our beliefs? Can we change our beliefs? How long does it take to change a belief? Don't our beliefs really dictate how we expect and perceive our lives to be? To me, a belief is merely a feeling based on our perspective of what we think is certain.

In one fell swoop, I will answer all the questions above with one example. About a month ago we purchased an antler chandelier for our home. It is constructed with eight mule deer antlers. It was my belief that the only way you could get antlers was by killing a deer and extracting them. I "felt" certain that was the only way. Then my seven-year-old son told me that our chandelier is constructed from what are called "shed" antlers. He went on to further explain that the deer actually shed the antlers and then grow new ones. I thought he was pulling my leg. He was not cracking a smile like he usually does when he's trying to put one over on me; he didn't back down when I challenged him yet I still doubted him and thought perhaps he was the one who was misinformed. I checked with my wife, and she matter-of-factly confirmed my son's explanation. This fact played a big part in her decision to get the chandelier. She would buy it only if it was made of shed antlers. In the meantime my son had grabbed a book that illustrated the cycle of growing and shedding antlers. Wow, I had been living a pretty long time with an incorrect belief.

That's only one of many examples. I am still discovering that I am guilty of living with incorrect beliefs, many of which are not the most empowering. So think about it. In only a matter of minutes after talking with my son and then my wife I gained new certainty about how antlers can be acquired. Minutes! Not months, years, or decades. It's really just a matter of having new and correct information, taking the old tape out and putting the new tape in, so to speak. It really happens quite quickly. The only reason it may take a long time to change a belief is that we believe it will take long and because we passively wait for the evidence to support a new belief rather than actively creating or finding the supporting evidence. Believe this—if you actively seek the supporting evidence for what you want to believe, you will find it. This fact is the key to changing your belief system to one that works for you instead of against you.

Some beliefs are deeply woven into or tangled up in our

behavior. This approach works the same with those embedded beliefs too. For example, take my definition of disappointment. It wasn't too long ago that I would get disappointed or depressed pretty dog-gone easily from just about anything not going my way or not being easy. I would catch myself saying things like, "Why does this have to be so difficult or complicated? Why can't this just be easy? This isn't going to work out? Why can't I be one of the lucky ones?" That, my friends, is what we call a Downward Spiral or a Doom Loop. Where do you think those usually cause you to end up?

When you ask yourself questions your brain searches for the answers. The answer becomes your focus. Change the questions you ask yourself and you change your focus. If you are asking the Doom Loop questions your brain comes up with all kinds of answers for that focus. Take the Doom Loop question of "why can't this be easy?" vs. the more empowering question of "how can I have fun doing this easily?" For each question your brain will come up with different answers. Which question would you rather have the answer to? If you persist in focusing on the Doom Loop questions, the result is usually one of crash and burn or a lifestyle that includes medication. I am not against medication if there is a chemical imbalance going on. However, here we are talking about a thought-thinking imbalance. I am not a doctor and please understand I am not prescribing here. Assuming that it is a thought-thinking imbalance that is the problem, the way to remedy it is with an Upward Spiral of thoughts and questions.

Try thoughts like:

- It may take me a couple of tries to get it right and that's okay.

- What am I learning as I work or play through this?
- How can I have fun doing this and enjoy the process?
- How great is it going to be once I complete this?
- I know I can do it; I've had other successes.
- What are the gifts associated to this circumstance?

It is a game my friends. The kicker is nobody gave you a rule book or a play book on how you can win the game. You see, it is your game. Who, then, should make the rules? There are certain rules you learn that enable you to exist in society and stay out of jail and above ground. There are certain rules of physics that you have to just accept. If you hold an apple three feet over the ground and let go, it will fall three feet and hit the ground ten out of ten times. It helps if you accept those kinds of laws and work with them. What I am suggesting is that you can change the rules you have created or accepted to live your life by. Those rules are basically built on your beliefs. So, when would be a good time to examine the rules you have set for yourself and determine if they empower you to win the game? How about now?

If you catch yourself saying something like, "It's not my rule or belief it's just the way life is," or "It's just a fact of life," or "That's just how I am," that's a pretty good indication that you are well entrenched with that belief or rule. If it is not serving you, you might want to adjust it. It is helpful to recognize your limiting beliefs. We live so deep inside of them; we often do not see them. One way to recognize a limiting belief is to notice how we answer these questions during times of adversity:

BELIEF REVEALER/REWRITER

I am ______________________________

and what that means is ______________________

____

____

So I ______________________________

____

-OR-

Life is ______________________________

and what that means is ______________________

____

____

-OR-

This (situation) is ______________________

____

and what that means is ______________________

____

____

People are ______________________________

and what that means is ______________________

____

____

The next step after recognizing what our limiting beliefs are is to delete them from our hard drive and install our winning beliefs. It is a conditioning process. Keep your focus on your new winning beliefs. Put the blinders on so you can no longer see, hear, or feel the limiting beliefs. Your winning beliefs will soon be your default.

RULE REVEALER

To reveal your rules, fill in the blanks:

In order for me to feel/experience ______________________

I must ______________________________________

and/or people must ______________________________

____

and/or the circumstances must be ______________________

____

-OR-

If ____

occurs/happens then I feel/experience ______________

____

-OR-

If others do/are ______________________________

____

then I feel/experience ______________________________

____

____

Download a free copy of this form by visiting www.ProBrilliance.com

Sometimes our rules are set up so that nobody could possibly win. Is your rule for being happy that you must be the richest person you know and have the body of a Greek God or Goddess and always feel in control and, and, and, and? Or is it something like, I am happy if I am here to take another breath. There is no universal rule for what happiness is for you. You make it up. So make it up so that it is easy to experience.

While we are at it, what does winning mean? What is winning to you? Is it what you want? Really? Or is it what Mom and Dad want? Is it what you think your college buddy or best friend wants? Is it what you think the last motivational speaker you heard wants? Is it what your favorite actor wants? What do you really want for yourself if you knew your answer was not to be judged by anybody, not even by you?

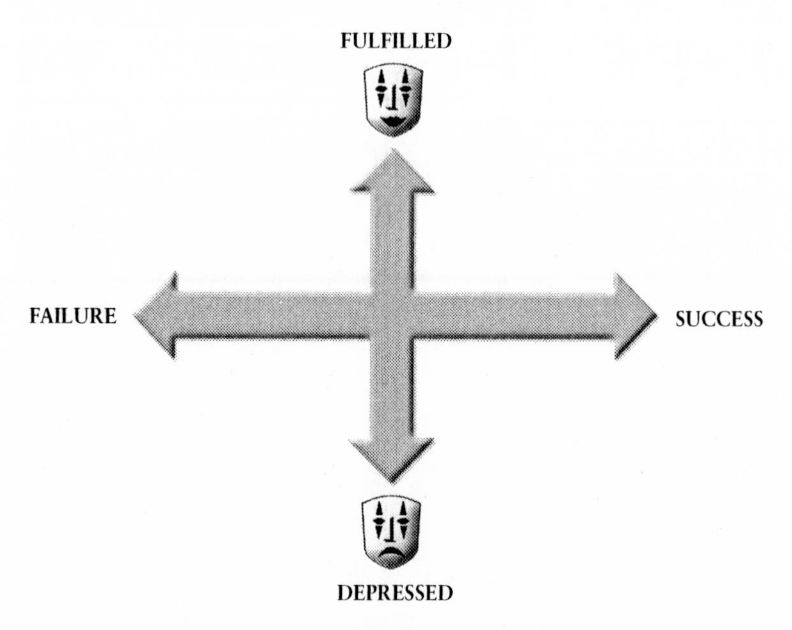

Figure 2 Fulfillment and Success

Be aware that there is a difference between success and fulfillment. Many people I meet have unconsciously melded the two together and think they are on the same line. One is a science and the other is an art. On Figure 2 Fulfillment and Success, plot your current experience of feeling fulfilled on the vertical axis and plot your experience of succeeding on the horizontal axis. Draw a horizontal line through the vertical axis at the point you plotted, and draw a vertical line through the horizontal axis at the point you plotted. Label the intersection of these two lines with (A).

Which quadrant are you in? Now put a (B) where you would like to be. If there is a difference, plot a line from where you are at (A) to where you want to be (B). To improve your position on the Fulfillment Axis, list three things you can do immediately to move up the scale. To improve your position on the Success Axis, list five things you can do to move in your desired direction.

Fulfillment Actions:

1. ______________________________
2. ______________________________
3. ______________________________
4. ______________________________
5. ______________________________

Success Actions:

1. ______________________________
2. ______________________________
3. ______________________________
4. ______________________________
5. ______________________________

Do you notice that your fulfillment actions are different than your success actions?

___

Were you aware of this before you played with this model?

___

What is one thing you have learned about yourself as a result of going through this?

___

___

___

___

___

This is the time to be true to yourself. If there ever was a time to be authentic with yourself, this is it. I have seen plenty of workshops, books, and programs that help people determine their values by providing a list of values and then instructing the person to choose what they think their values are. What ends up happening is people see all the admirable values that they think they should have for themselves and they create a list of values for their version of the ideal person. This approach to identify your values may work. I just don't think it's the best way to determine your very own current hierarchy of values. The more you understand yourself, your hierarchy of values, and your beliefs, the more clarity you will have in your life.

The easiest and best way to determine your values is to take a quiet moment and think about times in your life when you were totally happy, in the flow, in the zone, and unencumbered by all of the nonsense. If it is taking a walk out in nature and just getting away from it all, enjoying the fresh air and the natural beauty, then nature is one of your values. If playing with your kids gives you ultra joy, it's not too difficult to realize that spending time with your kids or being a fun and loving mom or dad is a high value for you. If doing a job well gives you tremendous satisfaction, then excellence is probably one of your values. Right now make a list of the experiences you really enjoy and what goes on during those experiences. What is the essence of these experiences? Be careful to not get caught up in gaining your satisfaction from others. An example of that might be something like feeling worthy only if my boss tells me I did a good job. You really have no control over your boss to say such things. Sure, it's nice when he does. However, you are marching down the path of setting rules that make your game harder to win.

Once you have made your list, ask yourself are you honoring your values? Are you spending time doing the things that give you the feelings you desire? If nature is one of your values, are you taking time each day to be with nature? What about your living area, does it include nature? If you have confusion in your life, I bet you are spending more time stepping on your values rather than honoring them!

My Values

To determine what you value most in life complete the following statements:

I feel most alive when I am ______________________

____

____

____

I am at peace when I am ______________________

____

____

____

I feel good about myself when I am ______________

____

____

____

I feel in control when I am ______________________

____

____

____

I feel great about my life when I am ____________

____

____

____

I feel OK when I am ______________________

____

____

____

I am at peace when I am ______________________________

____

____

____

I feel good about myself when I am ____________________

____

____

____

I feel in control when I am ___________________________

____

____

____

I feel great about my life when I am __________________

____

____

____

I feel most alive when I am ___________________________

____

____

____

Download a free copy of this form by visiting www.ProBrilliance.com

Try to come up with eleven. This will be your starting point in determining your values and their hierarchy. To determine the order of your hierarchy, ask yourself if you could only have one in your life which one would you choose. This becomes your #1 value. Of the remaining ten, if you could only have 1 more, which one would that be? That will be your #2 value. Of the remaining thirteen values, if you could only have one more, which one would you choose. You guessed it; that is your #3 value. Continue to do this for the entire list.

By identifying your hierarchy, you will gain an awareness of whether or not you are honoring your values in a given situation. It helps you make critical decisions that are right for you. It provides you clarity.

To move towards clarity start moving. That's right just get up and move. Many of my clients have health as one of their values. However, they get caught up like anybody else and start missing their workout times because they have certain deadlines at work or they have to do this or they have to do that. One, two, or three weeks slip by and they haven't worked out, and they are not conscious of why they are getting so cranky. I ask, "When was the last time you worked out?" All of the sudden the light bulb comes on. "Drop down and give me twenty!" I command. Amazingly, they do and in 30 seconds they actually feel better. Why? They are back on track with living a life honoring their values. Not their boss's values, not their parents' values, not even their third grade teacher's values. Theirs!

Whose life is it anyway? With over 62,250,000,000 people on the planet I don't think the master plan was for you or me to live someone else's life. Live your own life. Don't confuse this with serving others. I would highly suggest not living your life for someone else. To do so is to guarantee not living in alignment with your values. Even if among your values is caring for others, serving people, and being a good son or daughter, don't sacrifice living your values! You can live your values and fit in what makes you feel good. Hint: They are the same. Don't pretend that by not living your values you are helping somebody else. You aren't. The only way you can truly serve others is by you being totally authentic and living your values.

What if your values don't match up with your boss' or your company's values? Guess what? You are in the wrong company. Get out! It's that simple. There are plenty of companies and organizations that are looking for someone just like you. It may be they just haven't found you and you haven't found them yet. Since you are moving towards clarity you will most likely become aware of each other soon. That's just the way it works. At least that is my belief based on evidence I have seen in my life and in the lives of many other people.

Another well-meaning mantra often chanted by our tribe in an attempt to protect us is, "If you are going to do it, do it right (perfectly) or don't do it at all . . . be the best." It's true that somebody has to be #1. Why not you? Well, is that what you really want? While we are at it, what is "the best" and according to whom?

The great collegiate and Olympic wrestler Dan Gable lost only one match out of 183 in his prep and college career. He won the Olympic Gold medal in 1972 by not surrendering a single point to any of his six opponents. Is he the best or is the one person that beat him the best? Would a perfect wrestling career for Dan Gable be 183-0? Even in all the matches that he won, did he execute every move perfectly? Most likely not. However, he did execute most moves excellently and masterfully and that's what ultimately led to his victories. He achieved and continues to achieve excellence.

Do you know who the people are that do things perfectly?

They are the people who aren't doing much! They are usually the ones on the side lines watching and criticizing the masters.

All too often I hear people setting goals of perfection. I use to be one of them. Then I learned something that really changed my life. This is another rule of the game that you may wish to consider adjusting to make it easier for you to win the game. I am not talking about lowering your standards. Actually, it may even be raising your standards. One of my coach's caught on that I was always striving for perfection. Then one day he asked why I set such a low standard for myself? What was he talking about? I exclaimed, "Perfection is the highest standard!" Well, that's what I thought at the time. Realize that the illusion of perfection can keep you from living your life to the fullest?

Here's the distinction: There is perfection in what was, is and will be—true perfection, and then there is our notion of what should be—the illusion of perfection. There is a divine order. The power is in the truth that we always have the ability to choose a healthy perspective no matter what the circumstances. We may prefer that the circumstances be different. However, the circumstances are perfect since they are what they are. If they were to be anything else, they would be that something else. The reality is we are perfect just as we are where we are. Not to say we can't and don't change and grow. We do - perfectly. If we get wrapped up in the judgment that things should be different than what they are, it is easy to slip into thinking that things, people, and circumstances are not perfect. By judging, we move away from that which we have and want for ourselves. If you can manage your expectations and preferences of perfection and appreciate what currently is as perfect, you move toward what you have and want for yourself.

Inside each of us is the truth, our answers. Sometimes it needs to be coaxed or even shaken out of us. And here's what my coach coaxed out of me. Why is perfection the lowest standard of all? Because you will never ever achieve perfection as a standard that others and even yourself will agree on. It may be impossible. We all have different preferences of what should be. There will always be something that can be improved, tweaked, or made better per someone's expectation. This is not to say that what you do or create is not brilliant or excellent. It is and it is perfect since it is what is. Think about it. Whatever it is that you have done or created and take great pride in, couldn't it be tweaked just a little more? Couldn't you have run a little faster? Couldn't you have said it a little differently? Couldn't that brilliant report have been edited one more time? You really can't "could have" if you think about it. You can do, be, and have that something different next time out. You can't turn back the clock and do, be, or have it any other way than what it was. Thus, it was perfect. Don't get caught "shoulding" on yourself.

Many inventions are merely improvements on what was once considered something not perfect. Is the original not perfect anymore? Or was it the perfect original? Here is the point: Whether consciously or subconsciously you realize that if you set the standard of perfection for yourself, you will never really achieve it. As your awareness changes your preferences of what should be may change, and the illusion of "perfect" will continually elude you. You are "perfect" the way you are for this time. All that you do is perfect for this moment. You and any circumstance can not have been or be any different than what was or is.

Remember to choose a healthy perspective of the "what is." The take away from this is that perfection is not a standard of measurement. Become aware of your preferred standards and engage in achieving them from the healthiest of perspectives.

I am a recovering perfectionist—as if there really is such a thing as a recovering anything. I am here to tell you that now, after replacing perfection with the standards of excellence, brilliance, and mastery, the gates have opened wide and I have discovered a whole new world. I was one of those people that was always getting ready to get ready! That's the safe haven of the perfectionist. Not to say that great things haven't been accomplished by perfectionists. However, one purpose of this book is to expose you to ways to win the game. We agreed earlier that one of the elements to winning is feeling good about ourselves and what we contribute. Many perfectionists fail to reach that point in the game. They don't, or should I say, they refuse to enjoy what making such wonderful contributions can yield.

When you say the word "perfect" who do you think of? Perhaps not many if any. But when you ponder excellence, brilliance, and mastery, names like Michael Jordan, Tiger Woods, John Wooden, and Dan Gable may come to mind for the sports fan. Perhaps the names for you were Mozart and Beethoven, or Monet and Renoir. Get my point? It's not about chasing the illusion of perfection. It's about being the best you that you can be. Can you imagine a Bill Gates, Warren Buffet, Oprah Winfrey, Tiger Woods, or Muhammad Ali being anything else than what they are? Do you think Mother Teresa, Leonardo Da Vinci, Thomas Edison, or Abraham Lincoln would be as well etched in history and more importantly able to touch and positively influence the lives of so many people if they had done something else with their lives other than what they are best known for? Have the peace of knowing you are the perfect you the way you are right now.

They happened to discover their brilliance early in life and continued to develop it. They became masters. Were their efforts perfect? Were their contributions perfect? Were their accomplishments perfect? Perhaps not if judged by the preferences and expectations of others. However, their efforts, contributions and accomplishments were perfect since they are what they are. They couldn't be anything different otherwise they would have been. These are great people just like you and me. We undoubtedly associate greatness, mastery, and excellence with these people that had passion in the area of their brilliance and lived every day expressing it. The difference is that they recognized their own brilliance. What is your brilliance?

My Brilliance is: ______________________________

____.

Each of these people lived a philosophy of abundance, not of lack. These masters realized they could manufacture more of their brilliance for the world without limit. In fact it perpetually multiplied as they gave it away, so that they had more of it to give. They could not give it away fast enough. That is not going to happen if you have the strangle hold of perfection around your neck. It is so liberating not worrying about getting it, making it, creating it, saying it, building it, or showing it perfectly! It's already perfect. Now, just decide on your preference and advance confidently toward what you desire knowing that all is perfect along the way.

By giving yourself this kind of freedom from the illusion of perfection you will be amazed at what you do accomplish. You will go forth with a new perspective of what is possible for you. You will more easily recognize your brilliance and be able to embrace it with passion.

Take a moment now and list the things you feel you are great at doing and being. You can also list the things people tell you that you are good at doing. Go ahead! It may be a list of two or three things. It may be a list with over twenty things. They can be totally separate from each other or they can be variances of the same theme. Start to make a list. List as many things as possible.

Are you a good cook? Are you great with children? Do you have a knack for getting people motivated? Are you a good story teller? Can you take concepts that others seem to think are difficult and synthesize them into something really easy to understand? Are you a good driver? Do you enjoy driving? Remember that you don't have to get the list perfect. It is what it is for you. We are actually going for quantity at this point and not quality. We will organize it in a minute.

Go for it right now! Capture what you are good at and also what you really enjoy doing. Don't take anything for granted. Identify what is so easy and effortless for you that you assume everybody can do it; that is your brilliance. In fact not everybody can do what you do. If you knew today was your last day or this week was your last week what would you want to do? Next to each item, rank the ones that make you feel the best about yourself when you are doing them. You are on your way to discovering your brilliance and wrapping it in passion. This list contains the seeds that will bear the fruit matching the illustration on the package you've designed.

My Areas of Brilliance!

I am good at and enjoy:	**Rank 1–5**
1. ________________	______
2. ________________	______
3. ________________	______
4. ________________	______
5. ________________	______
6. ________________	______
7. ________________	______
8. ________________	______
9. ________________	______
10. ________________	______

Download a free copy of this form by visiting www.ProBrilliance.com

Chapter 5

By Contrast

"You have to leave the city of your comfort and go into the wilderness of your intuition. What you'll discover will be wonderful. What you'll discover is yourself."

— ALAN ALDA

How do you really know what you want for yourself? Oftentimes you may not. What helps in this case is a good dose of contrast. Become aware of what you don't want for yourself. You must be careful here not to dwell on what you don't want. Simply use the contrast to recognize or remember what you do want.

Here is what I mean. I am often complemented on how "together" I appear to be. When people learn of my background growing up, they really become curious about how I have managed to become successful. Let me share a little of my background with you so you'll understand. My family situation growing up is no worse and no better than any other. It was what it was. My parents loved me dearly. I knew this. However, when I explain my childhood, people remark how dysfunctional it was. I had no other reference until I started to visit other kids' homes and found things to be quite different from what was going on in my home. Communications were different, expectations were different, and behaviors were different at those other homes. Not necessarily better, but different. At my home, I felt totally loved growing up. There was no physical abuse of any kind, and there was no verbal or emotional abuse, that I was aware of.

I should actually say at my "homes." My parents were divorced when I was about a year old. Each of my parents came from extremely dysfunctional alcoholic families, and they used this fact as an excuse for flaring tempers and as an explanation for not knowing the right things to do as parents. For example, my mom would often say that nobody ever showed her, so how was she supposed to know. Unfortunately, my mom bought into the culture of male chauvinism and believed that a woman was simply to get married, depend on a man, and never think for herself.

In my marriage and family, I did not want to duplicate the life I had growing up. I saw how miserable and insecure both my parents were, and I knew I didn't want that for myself. Fortunately, I learned about contrast at a very early age. Granted it took me thirty years to realize what it was that I had learned. I was provided the gift of having a home life I didn't want for myself. By being well aware of what I didn't want, I was sure of what I did want by contrast. What have you just become aware of, in this moment that you really don't want for yourself? What is the contrast to that?

What I don't want is ________________________________

____

and therefore what I will have is _______________________

____.

Now begin to remove what you don't want from your life, from your focus and from your thoughts. Remove it and promptly replace it with what you do want.

What's your next step to moving closer to your desired reality?

I am willing to say NO to ___________________________
in my life, and I must say YES to ______________________

____

in my life in order to have ___________________________

____.

I tell you this not to impress you but to impress upon you that you always have a choice. If you are experiencing something you don't like chances are that the opposite is what you want. There are always two sides to the same coin. Take for example the two actuaries driving in the country. As they passed a cow on their right-hand side, one actuary commented to the other, "Look at that big brown cow." The second actuary responded with, "Well, at least he's brown on this side." The second actuary makes an important point. Do we really know the other side is brown too, or do we just assume?

All too often we are too smart or perhaps too lazy to ask more questions or be more curious to find out if there is another side. Now how limited is that way of thinking? That's assuming there are only two sides. How many sides to a cube? How many sides are there to a brilliantly faceted diamond? Explore the diamond called your life! Don't just find the flaw and focus on that. Chances are, if you explore all the other magnificent cuts, angles, and light you will lose track of the flaw. You will actually have to work very hard to find the flaw again. And why would you want to find the flaw anyway?

Don't dismiss contrast. Use it to your advantage. It is necessary. You can't have light without dark. You can't have joy without sadness. Without death there is no life! Turn the coin over, and find the preferable side. If there is something you want in your life that is not currently present, try focusing on that. This focus will attract it into your life.

Here is a little game you can play to see how focus affects your life. Look around your room or the environment you are in. Now notice everything that is brown. Take it in. Make a mental picture. Okay, now close your eyes, and when you open them again look only at this page as you read the following paragraph.

Keep your eyes set on this page and without looking up and around the room, in your mind recall where all the blue is. Did I throw you a little curve? Here is another curve, what did you hear or feel? Does this scenario remind you of the many times you have been focused on something and somebody asked you a question that you didn't hear? You probably have noticed by now that the only things you can recall about the room are the brown things – that's all you were focusing on.

You see, as magnificent as our brains are, they can only focus on one thing at a time. If I ask you to not think of an orange elephant, what immediately comes to mind? Who controls what your brain focuses on? You do! So grab the reins and put your very own foot on the accelerator. What color elephant do you want? Think it and it is done. See how easy that is?

So what is the brown in your life that you are focusing on? Change your focus and change your experience. Change your experience and your life has changed. Remember this: Life is about joy. It was not meant to be a struggle. Focus your thoughts on what you want, be present, and you will have joy now.

Find a role model or an existing representation of what you are seeking for yourself that contrasts with what you don't want. This can be anybody or any image. Perhaps it's a character in a movie. Maybe it's a sports figure or an actor. Maybe it's a teacher. Possibly it is a friend or parent of a friend. You don't have to limit yourself to just one. You can "borrow" various traits and behaviors from many different people to form the ideal you if you like. These role models are often referred to as mentors. Sometimes you know them and sometimes you just know of them. Sometimes they are directly involved in your life, and other times you are simply witness to theirs.

One of my mentors is my best friend's dad who didn't come into my life until my senior year in high school. Before I met him, I was pretty content with my choice to work at the local service station and forgo college. And then I was blessed with an introduction to his perspective of how the world works. This is a guy who was self-made and retired at forty-five to live in one of the most beautiful areas in the world, playing tennis, sailing, spending time with his family in the summer, and skiing with his family in the winter.

I am sure you would agree he has a pretty attractive life style. However, the challenges that this gentleman overcame to arrive at this life style were even greater than my own. It's interesting how only the "successful" self-made people admit it? Aren't we all self-made? Nobody ever refers to the miserable old crow as a self-made man, even though he is self-made just like the rest of us. All people are self-made. However, I am a big believer that no person is an island. We can't do it alone. Be proud to ask for help!

I witnessed and noted this man's great life style. Back then, I didn't figure that it was available to me. I had accepted my lot in life. Then I heard the story of his meager childhood and how he assumed full responsibility for his life, decided with total clarity what he wanted for himself, and set out to achieve it, accepting a "NO" from no one. In fact, this guy would shove the "no" back down your throat, making you enjoy its flavor as you choked it down. The dessert is all about possibilities.

He is what I refer to as a self-taught person. He did have a formal education, but more importantly he didn't often accept what he was being told or what he read at face value. He often would say, "Believe none of what you hear and only half of what you see." He would keep asking questions until he got the answer he wanted or needed. Very often, he would ask several different sources until he received the answer that worked for him and kept his momentum moving forward. Continuous momentum is paramount.

This guy would question everything. I am sure you have seen the bumper sticker that says, "Question authority." When I think of him, I am reminded of another bumper sticker that challenges, "Who are you to tell me to question authority?" Think about it for a moment. There is some definite contrast between the two, and yet they both suggest the same idea—think for yourself! Isn't that what so much of this comes down to? Who else can think for us? Nobody really. So, we are thinking for ourselves. But are we doing it consciously or just by default based on how our lives have unfolded to this point. Think for yourself. Think for the benefit of yourself. Think for the benefit of what you want for yourself.

Thinking comes out of curiosity and can yield confusion and frustration. Thinking through confusion yields clarity and understanding. And here you have once again progressed through the learning cycle from wonder to wisdom.

So what is your plan? Try this exercise on the areas of your life that you'd like to improve:

THOUGHT CALIBRATOR

A. Identify an area in your life that you'd like to improve.

____

____

____

____

B. Rank your current status in this area for improvement on a scale from 1 to 10 with 10 being the best. ________

C. If you had no fear or doubt and knew you would not fail, what must happen? What do you have to do to achieve a 10? ________________________

____

____

____

D. What are your current thoughts and excuses about why things are the way they are? What is the real reason you have not permitted yourself to have or do what is required in question C.? How must you change your thinking in order to achieve a 10 in this area of your life?

____

____

____

____

____

____

Download a free copy of this form by visiting www.ProBrilliance.com

Chapter 6

Your Own Screenplay

"Go for it now. The future is promised to no one!"
—WAYNE DYER

Practice, practice, practice. Do you remember the saying practice makes perfect? How about practice makes permanent? If you practice in bad form, the results may not be perfect, but they may become permanent. So let's examine our thoughts, evaluate them, and determine if they are right for us. Then, if we decide they are right for us, we can practice, practice, practice in good faith.

A great tool to get going in the right direction with healthy positive thinking is what is known as scripting. This is setting your intentions for your day by actually writing them out. This practice is an effective and fantastic way of starting your day with controlling your thoughts. I am not just talking about making a list of To Dos for the day. It is much more powerful. You will see results the first day you do it!

Here is how it works. Each morning take no less than 15 minutes and write out how you would like this very day to unfold. There are no limits here except for the ones you impose on yourself. Take off the blinders and go BIG! Think of it as if you are writing a movie script for your favorite character—you. Capture as much detail as you can. Really connect with your vision for the day. Get inside the script. See it, feel it, taste it, hear it, BE it! In other words think from your goals not of your goals.

It might go something like this:

> *I wake up on my own at 5:20 a.m. in my hotel room full of energy, feeling completely rested and refreshed. I am inspired and excited to work on my book for 30 minutes. I am confident that I will receive the most appropriate message to write about today so that I am on track with my life's purpose of provoking brilliance in others as well as in myself. I am so excited because I am well on my way to fulfilling one of my life's dreams of authoring a book that provides a message of hope and direction for others. I feel absolutely on track with my life.*
>
> *I finish 30 minutes of writing, and now I exercise to boost my energy for the day and feel good mentally, emotionally, and physically. It is a light workout. Simply three sets of seventy-five push-ups and three sets of fifty abdominal crunches. Upon completion I have a tremen-*

dous sense of accomplishment. I feel the blood pumping through my body, and I feel exhilarated.

I take the time to have a nourishing breakfast of three egg whites, wheat toast and fruit. I am feeling healthy, alive, and full of energy.

I head into the office where I coach two business executives, help them effectively launch their new businesses, show them resources and how best to build a marketing action plan and a prudent business plan. We spend five inspiring and creative hours together. My clients feel it is time very well invested. They see what is possible for their business and have a plan and direction once our sessions are done. They pay my rate and I accept it graciously. They feel great about the relationship and retain my services.

I call home and tell my wife about my exciting day. I listen enthusiastically as she shares with me the details of her and the kids' day. I let her know that I love her very much and am looking forward to seeing her in a couple of days.

I finish the day, head back to the hotel, and change into something more casual for my hour's journey north to see one of my best friends and his new family. We enjoy a wonderful dinner and share laughs, reflect on the good old days, brainstorm, and rouse excitement about the great new days now and ahead. I leave my friend's home with a deep sense of fulfillment and gratitude for the blessing of such a wonderful buddy. I am so happy and excited for him, his wife, and their baby girl.

I am proud of him, and I know he is proud of me. We are both thankful for the time together, and we look forward to the next time we can share the energy of reconnecting and simply being.

I return safely to my hotel and record this excellent day in my journal. I check my emails and respond accordingly. I check my list of To Dos and turn them into Ta Das. I call home to tuck everybody in, and then I go to sleep counting my blessings.

That is how scripting works. It's kind of like journaling in advance. It gives you a direction in which to travel for the day. Throughout the day, I remind myself what I scripted and this gets me back on track. It will work for you too. The key is to clearly focus on the feelings and the essence you want to achieve. Get yourself to feel as if you have it now! That is what it is all about—the good feelings. So be sure to include descriptions of those feelings in your script and really feel the feelings as you connect with your vision of the day.

Here is a mental and emotional conditioning assignment. Give yourself permission and commit to doing this for twenty-one days so that it can become a habit. You will be astounded at what will unfold for you. Many people I speak with have bought into a false assumption that they are not disciplined enough to do a daily practice. I am here to tell you that if you are reading this you have all the discipline you will ever need. It may be the proper habits that you lack. Make scripting a habit.

Chapter 7

Magnetic Master Mind

"How simple it is to see that all the worry in the world cannot control the future. How simple it is to see that we can only be happy now. And that there will never be a time when it is not now."

— GERALD JAMPOLSKY

Remember this: You are not given a thought without also being given the resources and fortitude to manifest it. The great Napoleon Hill said, "Whatever the mind can conceive and believe it can ultimately achieve."

What most of us need to work on is the believing part. Everybody gets flashes of brilliance of how they want to see themselves and experience life. We have all caught a glimpse of our life's greatness—a grander vision that calls us to release our false security and re-engage life. We begin to see life as a heart-beating, truth-telling, sweat-pouring, straight-from-the-gut adventure that makes us, and everyone around us, feel fully alive. Then the voice of the mind moster slips in and starts talking us out of what is truly and purely ours. It's important to know that the bigger the challenge or vision often means the bigger the mind master and the louder the internal critic.

Lots of practice is necessary to redirect our thoughts and silence the inner committee that extinguishes our passion. Remember the conditioning we talked about earlier? Can you think of anything else that may be more important in your life than taking the time to redirect your thinking? Let's face it, your life depends on it!

Perhaps this quote will inspire you and help you change your belief, allowing you to accept what you set your intentions on: "Therefore I tell you, whatever you ask for in prayer, believe that you have received it, and it will be yours," (Mark 11:24). How powerful is that? How very simple is that? In my opinion, the key word is "believe." So when you take your quiet time—whether it's prayer, meditation, journaling, or scripting,—immerse yourself in the sensations of what it would be like to actually have what you want.

You see, there is a difference between the wanting and the having. When you want something you are actually keeping it out there away from you. Consider this: Does a person who wants X have the same thing going on in their head, heart, and soul as a person who has X? No. The wanter and the haver are experiencing two very different realities regarding X. If you have a pencil in your hand, are you wanting the pencil or do you have the pencil? Right, you have it.

In the mental and emotional experience of your daily quiet-time practice, having in belief and imagination can and will precede having on the physical level. Wanting X and having X cannot occupy the same space. In wanting there is a twelve-foot pole out in front of you and at the other end of the pole is X. As long as that pole—the wanting—is between you and X, you will not have X in your life.

Wanting reflects lack. Wanting is not having. It can never be the same as having. However, once you collapse or remove the wanting there is nothing between you and X. So the crucial act of believing removes the wanting.

Getting back to the fifteen minutes of quiet, all you will need to do is daydream, fantasize, hallucinate what it is like to already experience X in your life. The form of your practice doesn't matter whether it's prayer, meditation, journaling, or scripting. The important thing is to quiet your mind and focus on the experience and feelings of having.

Scientifically speaking everything is a vibration. The only difference between forms is the speed with which they vibrate. Thought is simply a vibration. A thought or feeling of lack or wanting is a different vibration than the thought or feeling of having and enjoying. You are a magnet and your vibration or thought dictates what you attract into your existence. If you are always wanting and the vibration is that you want but don't have, then what do you think your magnetism is attracting? That's right! You are attracting exactly what you are focusing on—the wanting, not the having. By shifting your vibration—your thought—to having, X will be yours in no time. If you have a vibrating tuning fork and next to it you hold another tuning fork, in the same key, the second tuning fork will begin to vibrate without it physically touching the other. It resonates with the first tuning fork. The world resonates with your thoughts, bringing into your life exactly what you focus on.

If there is nothing between a magnet and a piece of steel to interrupt the force of attraction between them, they come together instantly. However, if there are things between the magnet and the steel that interfere with the force of attraction, then the magnet and the steel will remain apart. In the case of thought, the interference is the wanting; it's that twelve-foot pole between you and X. Remove the barrier, exercise strong thoughts and belief, and X will zoom towards you.

Become a "Happy Magnet" in your life. Here is how you can start. Shift and recalibrate your vibration to attract what is already yours and remove all the twelve-foot poles. Notice and remove your barriers, those pernicious and negative thoughts of lack. Whenever the negative thoughts and feelings of lack creep in, immediately eliminate them from your head, heart, and soul! Visualize it on a computer screen and hit the Delete key, and see those thoughts and feelings vanish. Say to yourself, "Cancel, cancel, cancel" as soon as they surface. Spray them with weed killer. Extinguish them with tidal waves of the positive! Do whatever you have to do. Do one, do them all. Just do something!

Remember, wanting is negative; it is an affirmation to the universe that you lack something. But the reality is that X exists; it is available to you. Have you made yourself available to it? You already have it. You must believe this just as you must breathe air to stay alive. Think from your goal rather than of your goal. Until you understand that you experience exactly what you focus on, you will not be moved to change your focus. It's that simple. Change what you focus on.

The following example from my own experience clearly illustrates the value and the challenge of choosing your focus. One late afternoon my family decided to go out for dinner to a local pizza restaurant that we enjoy. We gave my mom a call inviting her to go with us. She accepted. A few minutes after our food had been served and we were all well into enjoying our meals, my mom snapped at me to get my elbow off the table. In response, I reminded her that we were in a very informal setting. Well, she came back with another quip. Quickly recognizing what was going on, I simply let up and did as she wished. You see this is my mom's only area of perceived control over me. At this point in my life I have made a conscious choice to relax in a casual setting when I dine with friends and family. So rather than arguing with her over my dining posture, I simply made the choice to let her be right so that Mom would feel okay. From that point on in the meal, I did keep my elbows off the table.

Mom wouldn't let it drop. She stopped eating and said she had lost her appetite. As the meal progressed, Mom stewed, and then she announced that she was not speaking to me any more.

After paying the bill, we went out to the car and I tried to assure my mom that I meant no disrespect and that I was sorry. Again my purpose was to get her to feel okay about things and not to win the battle of the elbows. Gingerly, I asked what exactly it was that I had done to offend her. Enraged, Mom explained that I was lying on the table while I was eating my food, and that she had tried for thirty-nine years to get me to keep my elbows off the table. It took a lot of focused self-control for me to keep the agenda of trying to get Mom to "okay" versus letting her know of her current engagement in crazy-making. So, I said "I'll try to do better next time." She shot back with "don't try... just do it!" To which, keeping with the agenda, I said "okay, Mom, I'll do it."

During this event, there were several paths that could have been traveled based on each person's perspective or focus. My mom made a clear and simple choice. Instead of focusing on the happy components of the scenario—sharing a meal with her family—she chose to focus on the one thing that would cause her dis-ease, dis-comfort—my elbow on the table. Unfortunately, Mom didn't see that she had ultimate control over what she focused on and ultimately experienced. It is as simple as making a choice of what to focus on. This is huge folks! All of us have to work at choosing a positive focus. Again, it is a conditioning process. What that means is that it does get easier so hang in there.

Clear thoughts are stronger thoughts, and the stronger the thought, the stronger the power of attraction. So what does that mean? A clearer, stronger thought is the result of a fuller sense of what you are focusing on. The more sensory perceptions you can bring to your thoughts and imaginings, the stronger and more effective they are. By doing this you are calibrating your vibration to match the vibration of that which you desire. Clarity of sight, sound, touch, smell, and taste in your thoughts makes them powerful thoughts.

As an example of the four ways of getting what you desire, we can examine the simple process of acquiring a delicious dessert. So you have a craving for ice cream. The first way to fulfill your craving is for you to get up from where you are, go to the freezer, and get yourself some ice cream. The second way is to ask someone to get it for you, and they go get it and bring it to you.

So far this shouldn't rock anybody's world. The third way is you desire ice cream and someone happens to offer you some of theirs, or better yet surprises you with your own. Is it really a surprise? I know you already practice the first and second ways, and you have probably experienced the third way.

Most people would dismiss the third way as a coincidence. How do you define "coincidence"? To you, is it a fluke, luck, a rare occurrence with no cause and effect? Let's break it down. "Co" means with. "Incidence" means occurrence, frequency, or commonness. Let's use the meaning frequency. What frequency are you tuned into? The more you focus in on your ideal frequency, the more coincidence you will experience. Therefore, think of the word coincidence as meaning "with frequency." The more CoIncidence you can muster, the sooner you will be experiencing the fourth way. "What exactly is the fourth way," you ask? When you desire ice cream and it suddenly appears, you are experiencing the fourth way. Take heart, I'm still tuning my dial to that frequency too.

The music from the many different radio stations is floating around us on a multitude of available frequencies. The tuner or receiver must be dialed into just the right frequency to receive the music you desire to hear. If you are stuck on static or a style of music you don't care for, it's not that the music you desire doesn't exist, you just haven't tuned into it yet. Recalibrate your dial. Change the vibration. While tuning in, be sure to enjoy the different music you come across, and realize that the music is not held within the radio. If you start to get this you are well on your way to provoking your brilliance and bringing forth more of what you want for yourself in life.

Heads up! Once you get tuned into the station you like you will most likely travel out of the zone, and then you will need to surf the dial again. This is part of growing and discovering who we are and along the way you will be exposed to all kinds of music. Enjoy the process.

Now that you have your radio turned on, it is inevitable that you will experience more third-way and possibly fourth-way coincidences. As you do be sure to capture them here:

Date	Occurance / Way	Resulting action or insights
1.		
2.		
3.		
4.		
5.		
6.		
7.		

Now try this visualization and experience the power of your mind. You may want to have somebody read this part to you so you can bring full focus and concentration to the exercise and get the full experience.

Take a minute, close your eyes and really imagine yourself in your kitchen. Imagine getting a lemon. Hold the lemon in your hand and notice its texture. Feel its many dimples and its firmness. Bring it up to your nose and inhale the light lemon scent. Now set the lemon down on the counter or chopping block. Take out your favorite paring knife, you know the one; it may have a little nick out of the blade or perhaps the tip is broke off. Now place the knife on the lemon and cut it in half. Notice a little of the juice may be on your cutting board. Pick up one of the halves and gently squeeze it to bring more of the juice to the cut surface. Maybe some of the juice runs onto your hand. Now bring it up to your nose, and smell the aroma of the freshly cut lemon. Move the lemon to your mouth and bite into it!

What just happened? Did you begin to salivate? Using the power of your imagination, you got your whole body to respond. In that exercise of thought and visualization, your whole being was experiencing that lemon. In only a couple of minutes, you directed your body to action through thought.

As we established in a previous chapter, there are only two types of problems:

1. **We know what we want, but we don't know how to get it.**

-OR-

2. **We don't know what we want.**

So, what is the remedy to these problems? Make it up. Imagine it; make it happen just like you did with the lemon. That's it: thought, imagination, hallucination, fantasizing, recalling, daydreaming, that's the first step. Have a vision that creates a vacuum and pulls you forward. The second step is to take action by stepping into your vision and being willing to learn, grow, and blunder along the way. The people who do are doers, and doers make mistakes while making it happen. People who don't make mistakes don't do! They are what I call "Don'ters," and they are the Discouraged Dead Magnates of society.

Discouraged Dead Magnets (DDMs) are those people that have, in essence, given up on living the life they want. Their focus is on judging what is not right with their life and the world, rather than appreciating all the gifts with which they are blessed. They are not attractive in any sense of the word. When in your presence, they can alter or even block your attractiveness. They are an energy drain to themselves and those around them. They can be resurrected, and yet their belief is they cannot. So, their attitude is why bother? The first time something negative happens to someone they are perhaps a victim. Fair enough! The second, third, and fourth times, they are a volunteer.

DDMs are volunteers for living the life they don't want. They focus so much on what they don't want or don't have that they perpetuate their experience of lack. On some level, it serves them either by gaining sympathy or attention from others or perhaps providing them the false feeling of security of not having to take risks. They are the chronic complainers. Keep in mind that people only complain about things they believe should be different and are not willing to take the risks to affect change. Steer clear of these people. They can be highly infectious and contagious. You must avoid them at all costs.

What must you say "Yes" to in order to give yourself permission to make more mistakes and be a Doer?

I say YES to ____

____

____

I commit to avoiding the following "Don'ters:______________

____

____

____

____

Chapter 8

A.C.T. Your Goals

Advance Calmly Towards

"Endeavor to be what you desire to appear"
—SOCRATES

You must make it a habit to spend no less than fifteen minutes each day, preferably in the morning hours, architecting your life. Spend no less than fifteen minutes in the evening capturing the accomplishments of the day as well as seeking clarity around tomorrow. This practice frees your subconscious to access your cast of thousands as you sleep providing you the answers and guidance necessary to live your vision. Did I just hear you say you don't have the time to do that? Isn't the rest of your life, your happiness, and your family's happiness worth those moments of planning and reflecting?

Acting means doing, getting the momentum going, and overcoming inertia. This is the next step—action follows thought. The universal law of physics tells us that an object at rest will remain at rest until a force is brought or transferred upon it. It is my intention that this book and message will be the catalyst to propel you to take effective action.

If your life is not where and how you want it to be, chances are you have been taking less than desirable action or your effectiveness is questionable. If you are looking for a sunset, it doesn't matter how fast you run toward the east; you will never see the sunset.

One of my coaches Robert Stuberg says, "The quality of your life is in direct proportion to your ability to handle uncertainty." Tony Robbins says, "The quality of your life is in direct proportion to the quality of your communication." Both of these are so true, and I add that the quality of your life is in direct proportion to action that you plan for yourself and then implement.

Results = Activity X Effectiveness

I see so many people taking lots of action in their lives. Working 60+ hours per week, they are involved in more clubs, organizations, and teams than there are hours in the day, it seems. Working so hard at a job and a life and yet there is a feeling of emptiness. Believe me, if hard work was the answer, ditch diggers would be the most well-off people on earth. Think about it for a moment. The most well-rewarded people in our society are not the ones performing back- breaking labor nor are they those who are the smartest or make their living just thinking. It is the person who THINKS and can apply that knowledge—act—in a way that provides value to others who is well-rewarded. Often times THINKING can be nothing more than asking yourself and others questions and capturing the data and then looking again at the problem, challenge, or situation with a newly defined perspective or awareness and voilà, a solution surfaces. Within every situation is the answer. We just need to equip ourselves with the right resources and perspective and tune in to the right frequency to be able to receive it.

Okay, you have thought things through as best you can. You have scripted out what you intend to have, feel, and experience. Next, act on it. Since you put some thought into it, scripted it out getting all of your senses involved, taking action won't be such a challenge. You have already gone through it in your mind. As far as your mind is concerned you have really already done it. So much of our reality, if not all of it, is in our minds.

How many times have you put yourself through the worst possible scenario in your mind, only to be relieved that the worst did not happen and perhaps you were even delighted with the outcome? In your mind and in your body, the Bull Scenario or BS was real. It caused your blood pressure to rise, your heart to pump, and on and on. We can expend so much time and energy allowing life to pass on by, the next thing you know you are in your rocker looking back on your life wondering what happened.

There are three types of people. Those who make life happen, those who watch what happens, and those who wonder what happened. Who do you want to be?

A hero dies only once. A coward dies a thousand deaths—in his mind. And in the coward's mind it is real. This ultimately affects all aspects of life, health, and well-being. By controlling your thoughts, playing boldly, and taking more risk you build up immunity to the inner deaths. You can then live invincibly. What would you do differently if you were invincible? What is one thing you will start doing differently right this moment to live your life the way you want? ______________________________

____

____

____

____

____

Start living your life invincibly. It's as simple as controlling your thoughts! Simple though not easy. You have had years of conditioning. You don't just go the gym once and workout and claim you are in shape. It takes time. You need to condition the muscles. In this case it is the thinking muscles. Once you build these muscles you can kick the krap out of the mind monsters too.

While I was facilitating a leadership conference, during one of the evenings after dinner many of the participants headed up to the local sports bar of the resort property. It was about 10:30 p.m. and everybody was having a good old time. Some were dancing, others were playing pool, and others were conversing. Suddenly the festive ambiance was brought to a screeching halt as the focus swung towards one of the partygoers who had collapsed. As he lay on the ground staring lifelessly at the ceiling, those near him screamed, "CALL 9-1-1!"

The words "heart attack," "stroke," and "seizure" floated through the silence. Most people feared the worst. I didn't allow my mind to stay there; I felt it was not a life-threatening situation.

Yes the worst case popped into my head, but I was immediately doing some quick perspective work in my head. I ran a bunch of other possible scenarios; maybe he simply passed out from fatigue; maybe he drank a little too much; maybe he lost balance from the tall stool, toppled over and fell hitting his head and knocking himself unconscious. By this time the EMTs finally showed up, strapped him to an oxygen tank, loaded him on the gurney, and whisked him away to a hospital.

As it turned out, he had just suffered from fatigue. He was back in class the next morning bright-eyed and ready to go.

Many people had feared that he had suffered a heart attack and was on his way up the channel of light. Those that were close to him were on the verge of hysteria only because of what they were allowing their minds to focus on. The news the next day was a relief to everyone. However, in the absence of facts, these people had put themselves through the worst. During that episode, their ability to deal with the uncertainty of the situation degraded the quality of their life to hysteria. Their heads, hearts, and souls were on the roller coaster of the emotional devastation with thoughts of losing a friend and colleague. Their internal communication was creating the worst. Their communication with those around them was heated and antagonistic. These people were feeling out of control.

So much of our self-talk is fear based arising from uncertainty. So if our self-talk is just that—stuff we say to ourselves—we can decide what to say to ourselves. Let's speak to ourselves in a way that gives us back the control. So what does that sound like? All we are doing when we are feeling out of control is asking ourselves what-if questions that we don't have the answers to. We make up answers, and we tend to talk ourselves down a scary road. It usually goes something like this: What if our company gets bought? And what if they eliminate our department? And what if I can't find another job? And what if I can't make the mortgage payment? The simple fix is to continue with the "what-if" questions and take the high road. You may need to make it up, that's what you're doing anyway.

Make it up the way you want it to turn out. It might go something like this: What if we get taken over by a great company? And what if they need a department such as ours? And what if I end up getting a promotion? And what if I actually become the head of the new department? This too is a conditioning process. Recognize when you don't have control of the situation and regain your control through your thoughts.

"WHAT IF…" CALIBRATOR

(A) What are three areas of your life that are causing you some anxiety?

1. ______________________________
2. ______________________________
3. ______________________________

(B) What are some negative what-ifs you catch yourself thinking for each of these three areas you listed in (A)?

1. ______________________________
2. ______________________________
3. ______________________________

(C) What are your new and more empowering what-ifs around each of the situations in (A)?

1. ______________________________
2. ______________________________
3. ______________________________

How do you feel now about those three situations that were causing you anxiety? ______________________________

____

____

____

____

____

Download a free copy of this form by visiting www.ProBrilliance.com

Don't concern yourself with taking misguided action. You have set yourself up for just the opposite—guided action. The thinking and scripting that you have done is like locking in a flight plan at take-off. The plane has a path to follow and so do you. Trust yourself! You will not stray. Thinking and scripting are ways of taking action. And now you are ready to step up the volume of your action. If you have set up your rules so that you can easily win, then you won't fail by taking action. For me the only way to fail is to give up and not learn anything. Well, I don't give up too easily and I always learn something. Failure can be summed up as not ever getting the intended result, something equal, or something better. Notice I didn't say not getting the intended result on the first try. My rules make it nearly impossible to fail. Whose rules for failure have you adopted? Do you have to get it right the first time? If that is the case, I wish you lots of luck!

A big part of action is just giving yourself permission to get it wrong and perhaps even look foolish. If you get it wrong, you are still getting results. You are getting data; you are learning. You have become clearer about how not to do it. On the next attempt, try something different. Often times it is only a little adjustment that needs to take place. Please do yourself a favor. Don't continue to do the same thing over and over and expect different results. That is simply insanity!

If you don't already have a solid trust in yourself, developing that inner trust will serve you well. Trust that you have an overriding intention to take care of yourself—you do. Take each situation or present moment for what it is rather than collecting all kinds of different situations—past and future—into one big incoherent mess.

You are probably already trying to see each situation in its own light. Are you doing it in the most empowering way possible? If you were to stop and write down all the stuff that is going on in your life, your city, your state, your country, and the world, and you constantly bounced your focus around all of the craziness and chaos, you would become literally paralyzed with fear. You really do have a choice of what you decided to focus on. The world is going to continue to spin. Where you let your mind wonder is what determines the contents of your mind.

What you saw on the news last week, did it really affect you and your immediate world? Did you have to change the way you were doing anything as a result of what was broadcast. Did it really change your awareness? For that matter, can you even remember what was on the news last week? The broadcast was really only a snippet, a tiny little glimpse of what went on in the world that week, wasn't it? However, just like everybody else who watched it, you went through the emotional roller coaster. Your focus for that period of watching the news was totally outside of you and on something that you pretty much don't have any control over.

What if you focus your attention on your own broadcast and replay it over and over? I call this "focusing your focus," and it can put you back in control faster than anything else you can do. Focus on what is good and will be good in your life. Crank up the volume and brighten the picture. This will serve you well. Don't worry about missing something that might be important and may affect you. If it is important enough that you must take action for protection or prevention, you will get the news one way or another. Somebody will either tell you or ask you about it. It will interrupt your chosen focus. It will find you.

Focusing your focus can be equated to deciding what to point your video camera at while at a party. To illustrate this point, let's take two cameras into a party. You get one and I get one, and then we'll take it to a friend who wasn't there and let them get sense of what went on by viewing the videos.

Here's what your camera captures: Children playing; a couple guys reminiscing about the good old days and people gathered in the kitchen eating hors d'oeuvres and drinking wine.

Here's what my camera captures: The great view out over the deck, sweeping from left to right and then stopping on a couple having a quiet yet spirited debate.

Now we play the two movies for our friend. Is she going to think that our movies were taken at the same event? Most likely not. But they both were. Which one is the more accurate representation? Both are accurate. All the captured events were going on at the same place, but each camera was focused on something different. These two cameras captured only two perspectives. How many others did we miss?

In any situation, all perspectives are accurate. Which is accurate for you depends on what your perspective is and what you are focusing on. If you don't like what you see simply move your focus to something you do like. You are in total control of where you point your camera. You can't possibly capture everything that is going on. So, be selective with your focus. Why not eliminate what is negative and unempowering and instead focus on what is positive and empowering. Point the camera at the good stuff.

How are you going to remember this concept? What will you

do to remind yourself to focus your focus when you find yourself with your camera pointed in the less than desirable direction? Think about it, and write your plan here:

My plan for focusing my focus is: ______________________

____

____

____

____

____

____

____

____

____

____

"When we walk to the edge of all the light we have and take the step into the darkness of the unknown, we must believe that one of two things will happen. . . There will be something solid for us to stand on, or we will be taught to fly."

—FRANK OUTLAW

Chapter 9

The Importance and Practice of Finding Your Answers

"The pain of regret far outweighs the pain of discipline."
—JIM ROHN

Keeping a journal captures the substance and breakthroughs of your life. It gives you the opportunity to listen to yourself. It allows you to reflect and to project. Ask yourself the empowering questions and avoid the doom questions. Here are a few examples of how to keep your questioning above the line:

Try: *How can I have fun and achieve?*
Instead of: *Why can't I achieve?*

Try: *What is the real opportunity here that I may be missing?*
Instead of: *Why can't things just go smoothly?*

Try: *How can I make even more time for this?*
Instead of: *Why is there never enough time?*

As answers and ideas come to you, write them down .You have all the answers. Accessing them can be the challenge. Earlier, we established the importance of thinking for yourself. In your journal is where you capture the thinking. It reinforces the lessons of your day and houses your brilliance for later reference and as a source to turbo charge your life. Do your scripting and your journaling in the same place. Try scripting in one color and journaling in another.

Initiating your journal is fun. At the beginning of your journal, make a numbered list of twenty-five things that would make your life excellent! You can list things to be, things to do, things to feel, things to acquire, things to experience, places to visit, and so forth. They may be related to income, relationships, health, or whatever you prefer. In the description of each, be sure to include the feelings you experience in relation to each one. For example, if having $100,000 in the bank is on your list, ask yourself how would that make you feel. Let's say it makes you feel secure. Then ask yourself what does feeling secure do for you? You might come up with, "I am not stressed over bills," or "I could buy what I want when I want." Then ask yourself again what does that do for you? After this type of investigation, you may come up with the feeling of peace of mind, or a sense of purpose, or clarity. You will know what it is when you get to it.

This is the core feeling you want to capture. Circle or highlight it in your journal.

You will soon realize that in your list of twenty-five desires you have captured perhaps four or five core feelings you wish to experience on an ongoing basis. These core feelings are what you are ultimately pursuing—not the specific thing, relationship, or place.

With this new awareness of what it is you are actually after, you have gained clarity. Just having this awareness will miraculously move you closer to having those feelings on a more frequent basis. This inaugural list can serve as a list of guiding principles when you write in your journal and script out your days. The perceived obstacles, problems, and challenges you thought you once had will become less intimidating. They may actually fade away. This was always possible. The difference is that now you have a new perspective—one of more clarity. Take a minute or two during each of your writing sessions to experience those core feelings. Get yourself into the state of actually experiencing them just like you did when you imagined the lemon. By doing this you are flipping the switch to your magnetism and amplifying your attraction.

To prove to you that you can do it, try the following exercise. It demonstrates how to bring those core feelings home. For this exercise we are going experience the feeling of total peace of mind. Was that one of the feeling on your list?

Take in several deep breaths and clear your mind as best you can. Let go of the day. Let go. Now think of a time you had total peace of mind in your life. Even if it was for only a short time; think! If for some reason you can't think of a time, make one up, and then imagine what it would be like to have total peace of mind. Notice how you feel; what is your breathing like? What are you noticing? What are you remembering? What sensations are you experiencing in your body? Just enjoy this feeling. Let it last as long as you wish.

So what just happened for you? What did you experience? Did you experience some peace of mind? In just a matter of minutes you achieved peace of mind for yourself. Did anything outside of you change? Did your bank account suddenly multiply by ten? Did all of your bills suddenly get paid? Was the car of your dreams instantly parked in your driveway? Did you get a raise? So, those are not the things that create a sense of peace—rather it's your mind that does it.

None of those external things really affect our feeling, our state of mind, or our lives. It's how we respond to them that affects our feelings and states of mind. We can be in total control of ourselves. We need to remember to regain control as you did in the peace of mind example. The more you can do this internal practice, the more the desired external manifestations will occur. Keep the faith. This internal practice along with guided action—not misguided action—will create your ideal life.

As the peace of mind and juicy lemon examples prove, you can experience real emotions and sensations in response to what is in your mind. You don't need to wait until something outside of you occurs or appears. You can have total peace of mind right this minute. Do you think you are more attractive to what you want for yourself when you are in a state of calmness and peace of mind or in a state of stress? It works from the inside out, not from the outside in.

It is merely a matter of developing the habit of not getting distracted. Do you need discipline to build a habit? Not really. You just need to raise your standard to what you want until it becomes a habit. In order to do that, simply create the right environment. You can do this by placing reminders for yourself to remember what you want to have, what you want to be, and what you want to do rather than allowing the fire hose of the day to wash those thoughts and intentions away.

Here's some help on this: Take the word cognizant. To be cognizant is to be aware or mindful. To recognize is simply to be aware again—to be mindful again. If it is true that repetition is the mother of skill, then you must be mindful—fill your mind—again and again and again and again and again with what you want for yourself continually throughout the day, week, month, year, and yes your life! Journaling is great for recognizing and remembering what you want.

Writing it down will affect you profoundly. Capture your life in your journal and life will lovingly capture and rescue you. Review it regularly! The best chapters of your life have yet to be written!

Make it a habit. For the next twenty-one days take the time to think, script, take action, and write in your journal and you will be amazed at how your life transforms. The great news is you will experience the benefits well before twenty-one days, but go the distance until it becomes a habit.

Another technique that will help you focus your focus and experience those core feelings is the use of Game Peaces, motivational reminders of who you are and what you do. They can be anything that you have read, heard, or were exposed. Record the information on an index card. Put the index card in a place that you encounter on a fairly regular basis. For example, I put Game Peaces in a folder with my pending bills. I only open this folder two or three times a month; seeing the messages of my Game Peaces every single day would diminish their motivational effect. I have Game Peaces in all sorts of places at work, at home, in the car, and throughout my environment. They are not plastered all over the walls. In fact if you came to my home or office you wouldn't know they are there. Only I know where they are hidden. Sometimes I forget about them until I run across a hiding place. Then when I see one, it fills my mind with the inspirational thought and feeling it was intended to invoke.

Unless you turn the light on you can't see what's already in the room. If you haven't turned yourself on, you can't see what you already have in your life. And you can't see how to bring things into physical reality within your life. For me, Game Peaces are a fun way to remind me again of the feelings that turn me on, keeping me magnetized and attracting what is mine. Take a few minutes and create some Game Peaces for yourself and be mindful of what you already know is great about you and your life!

Remembering what is important in your life feeds your fire to continue. You will be more likely to not pass up opportunities. And living this way will result in a life of fewer regrets. We usually don't regret much of what we do. It's what we haven't done that makes for regrets.

What is one thing you haven't done or the one chance you haven't taken that would leave you with regret, if yesterday was your last day on earth?

I wish I had done/taken/seen/tried/given/experienced: _______

____

____

____

____

____

____

As David Allen so eloquently puts it, "Let's face it...the only reason we complain about things is because we assume things could be different than they currently are, we just aren't willing to take the risk to make them so." What do you catch yourself complaining about? Perhaps it's time to take the risk and make a change. If you are not willing to take the risk to change, then build a bridge and "get over it." Otherwise take the risk and dump the regrets.

Here's the good news, you get another chance to make a different choice today. Remember, nobody has a lease on life. Life is now! It's not tomorrow, next week, next month, or two years from now. It's today! You want to change, right? Just not today! What gives you the audacity to think that you can put it off? Every day that you have to take another breath is the greatest gift in the world. Are you too busy throwing away the present with the wrapping in search of tomorrow's gift, or do you recognize that today is the awesome gift that you have? Appreciate it by using it now! Counting your blessings is one of the most powerful tools of clarity in your existence.

Have you heard the saying, "Work as if you will live forever and play as if you only have today"? What I take from it is the advice to structure my life so that I enjoy every moment as much as possible. Ideally, this structure includes setting up the right environments and making a living by doing work that you love.

I'm sure you've heard the saying, "Do what you love and the money will follow." When I didn't have money, I was preoccupied with that fact. I was focusing on what I did not have. Then I changed my focus and let go of the preoccupation with not having enough money. I started engaging the experience of what it would feel like having money and living that lifestyle and what that would ultimately expose me to. The result is that money found me. You see, it's not that the money was not available to me. It's that my focus on lack made me unavailable to the abundance.

Take this fact into every cell of your being: Abundance—financial abundance, abundance of loving relationships, spiritual abundance, abundance of health, abundance of resources—is in bountiful supply. There is enough of all of it for everybody. It's really simple. It's like a smile. Do you ration your smiles? Do you worry about running out or depriving others of theirs if you smile too much? You just make more, right? Or how about health; if you have good health does that take health away from someone else? On the contrary, health is a result of thoughts and choices made, eating right, exercising, life style, and the like. Financial health is similar. It is a result of right thinking, providing value for others, and awareness of our perceived value.

Is one of the things on your inaugural list of twenty-five things that would make your life excellent to get out of your dead end job, change careers, or perhaps start your own business and do what you really want to do? It may be something else entirely, but whatever it is make sure you have it written down. Capture it for now. Once you have identified what it is you want to accomplish, ask yourself what it is costing you by not having accomplished or at least attempted what you really want to do? Take a moment to really think what it is costing you emotionally, spiritually, physically, and financially. What are you going with out? What are you not enjoying? What are you tolerating?

I want to accomplish: ______________________________

____

____

____

____

____

____

____

Not doing so or attempting to do so is immediately costing me:

____

____

____

____

____

____

____

____

Now, record all the greatness and grandeur you will experience by doing what you really want to do? Don't let the mind monster sneak in on this one. Really get into it. Develop as much

detail as you can, illustrating what you will experience as a result of having gone for it and accomplished it. Write it with conviction as if you know in your bones you cannot fail. Remember those rules you set up to allow this to happen? Write down all that you would experience by giving yourself permission and going for whatever it is you really must have in your life.
By going for it and accomplishing my goal of what I really want for myself, I will immediately experience the following:

____

____

____

____

____

____

____

____

You should have a pretty exciting list. If you don't, then ask yourself is this really what I should be going for? Do I really want it for myself? It may not be, and that's okay. You have gained some clarity around what you can free yourself from. Perhaps, you started with a goal that wasn't even yours. Maybe it was Dad's goal for you. Maybe it was something you thought you should do to win back the ex-girlfriend from five years ago. What? Has it been that long already and you are still hanging out hope? And you are doing this because...? Please remember, this is all good, out of confusion comes clarity.

Pick one of the items that you successfully identified as something that is to be part of the mosaic of your life going forward.

You have a list of what it costs you, and you are clear you don't want anymore of that expense. You have a list of all the goodness it will provide you and fill your senses with by going for it. Now, who do you have to be in order to live it? What are the characteristics, knowledge, skill sets, or talents you must posses in order to have it? You know the drill by now—write it down. Don't worry if you think you don't have those qualities. I am here to tell you that you do. They just may not have revealed themselves to you quite yet.

Who do I need to be in order to go for it and accomplish my goals? (what are the qualities within me that I want to bring forward?)

____

____

____

____

____

____

____

What is your plan? Sometimes you need to travel light and not pack everything before you leave for your journey. If you packed everything you probably couldn't get out the door. Don't get stuck in the getting ready to get ready cycle while the game is going on. This is where some trust comes in. Trust yourself and trust that you will get what you need just when you need it.

A great example of how this theory works is the process of producing this book. For years I have said I wanted to write a book. And years went by—flew by, now that I think of it. I kept waiting, waiting, waiting. I made some feeble attempts here and there but never really committed to it. Then finally I decided and committed to unleashing the wisdom within me. I don't intend to sound masterful or all-knowing, but rather I want you to know that we all have it in us. You just need to tap yours.

Once I heard that we all have a book inside of us, I was able to grant myself permission to be an author, and the book started to unfold. I had been working with a new coach for about four months. We had great conversations, and after we hung up I was excited for about a day, and then the magic would start to fade. I caught myself continually negotiating with myself about continuing with him. I didn't seem to be moving toward any of my goals. I thought I would be "fixed" by now. I thought I would have this ball of tangled yarn called life all untangled by now. Then on our last call, he told me the story of Earl Nightingale who wrote a book called the Strangest Secret. One early morning, Earl woke up with an idea. You and I have had similar experiences, but Earl did something different. Rather than kidding himself that he would remember later when he got up for the day, he got out of bed. Put on a pot of coffee and started to write, write, and write some more. And by noon that day he had recorded his book, which is an all-time classic and best-seller.

Well, interestingly enough, the next day after I heard that story, I woke up at 3:00 a.m. with an idea for a book. It wasn't like it was all nice and neat in my head it was just a couple thoughts and the new reference of getting out of bed right away to capture it now instead of going back to sleep. So, I got up out of bed right then, put on a pot of coffee, and flipped on the computer. I managed to bang out sixteen pages. And I committed to spending at least fifteen minutes each day for at least twenty-one days writing my book. And see, here it is—proof that I stuck with it, and you can do it too.

Each morning I wake up not aware of what the heck I am going to write about. However, by the time I sit in front of the computer, I get a flash of brilliance! It may be something that occurred yesterday that reminds me of something, or I may glance at my bookshelf which triggers something within me. Often times, I just start reading what I wrote the day or two before and start expanding on it. I get what I need to fulfill my commitment to myself, because I trust in my bones that I will.

State Your Desired Outcome. Make it SMART. (Specific, Measurable, Actionable, Realistic, and Time bound): ________

____

____

____

____

____

____

It is common that people don't achieve their goals, because they don't know the next action to take in order to move in the direction of accomplishment. It may be as simple as getting a phone number or doing some research on the Internet. It may be pulling materials together or starting to save money. The important thing is to consciously recognize what must happen next in order to get to the next action, to the next action, and to the next action to eventually complete the goal.

Identify the next seven actions needed to do in order to move closer to accomplishing your desired outcome:

My Next 7 Actions

My Desired Outcome (Goal)

1. ____________________

____

By when: ____________________

2. ____________________

____

By when: ____________________

3. ____________________

____

By when: ____________________

4. ____________________

____

By when: ____________________

5. ____________________

____

By when: ____________________

6. ____________________

____

By when: ____________________

7. ____________________

____

By when: ____________________

☐ Yes! I commit to do whatever it takes, legally, morally, and ethically to accomplish this goal. I will steadfastly honor my values and use this goal as direction to living happily. I will not give up in the face of adversity. I know that all situations serve me, and I will learn from them on my way to succeeding!

I may need to say "No" to some things or some people in order to get what I want just as I will need to say "Yes" to some others. I give myself permission to do so.

I will notify ________________________________
(accountability buddy) by phone/e-mail/in person as I progress through each action item listed above.

Date ________________________________

Signature ________________________________

Download a free copy of this form by visiting www.ProBrilliance.com

You will most likely need to take more than just the initial seven in order to accomplish your goal, but let's keep it simple and start with the first seven. Chunk each set of actions to no more than seven and focus on those seven. Seven is your magic number. This will be sure to eliminate feelings of overwhelm. Make copies of the form as needed.

Now, are you ready? Are you willing to do whatever it takes to get it done? If you didn't answer this one with a resounding "YES!", then we have some more work to do on the preceding questions.

Chapter 10

Choice Attitudes

"Whoever commands their inner dominion directs the outer manifestation of their reality through proper and appropriate perception."
—MACHEN MACDONALD

I hope by now you are starting to recognize a pattern here. There is an inside world and an outside world. We may have some influence over what occurs in the outside world. There is obviously the law of cause and effect in the outside world. I am not so sure we have control of what goes on in the outside world. All too often we start to think this game called life is about control. "If only I could control or be certain of the outcome of what goes on outside of me then things would be alright." What happens is that things start going our way on the outside. At least that's what we think. We negotiate a good deal; we experience synergy with someone, or we are able to influence others to see our point of view; then all of the sudden we start kidding ourselves that we are in control of what is going on around us and in our lives. So, if we are not really controlling the outside world, what is it that we can control?

Dominion is what we must seek and strive to control. "Dominion" is an interesting word, meaning power and territory. The connotation I find empowering is power of the territory—control of the mind, the internal territory. The illusion is that we can control the outside world. But, it is only over our dominion—our inner territory—that we are King or Queen. As players in the game of life, we can set the rules for our own life by having dominion over our thoughts. Knowing and owning this control, we eliminate fear and win at our own game.

Attitude, attitude, attitude. Attitude determines your altitude. Attitude is everything. Attitude is the result of an emotionally charged belief. Regarding attitude, Ralph Waldo Emerson says, "To different minds, the same world is a hell and a heaven." Webster's definition describes it, "1. A bodily posture showing mood, action, etc.; 2. A manner showing one's feelings or thoughts; 3. One's disposition, opinion, etc." The dictionary verifies our claim that attitude is a matter of feelings, thoughts, and opinions.

Attitudes are formed in one of two ways. First, an attitude may be copped. Second, an attitude may be adopted. So what does it mean to cop an attitude? The word "cop" comes from the Latin word capere which means to take. Usually it implies taking something hastily or stealing quickly. With this definition in mind, by "copping an attitude" you are quickly taking something—that perhaps isn't even yours—without thinking about it.

It happens in an instant and is often reactionary.

Although it is a popular belief that the world causes one's attitude, my belief and my experience tell me that attitude is a choice. We always have a choice in how we think, feel, respond, act, and communicate. Making a choice requires an awareness of the options, whereas we are most likely to default to auto-pilot reactions, leading us to cop an attitude. Then we act and react from that attitude.

Next time you feel the situation is driving you, slam on the breaks and stop to evaluate the situation before traveling on. Ask yourself some questions like, "Is this really the way I want to be acting, or is there a better more enjoyable way?" and "What am I giving up by copping this attitude?" Go easy on yourself in the beginning. You may have developed a few habits with these attitudes that you regularly cop. You can change those habits by choice.

What's different about adopting an attitude instead of copping one? The word "adopt" implies the execution of thought and conscious decision. To adopt is to make a conscious choice. Just as copping can happen in an instant so can adopting. To gain this speed with adopting just takes practice. The brain is the quickest most amazing computer there is, and giving it a replacement program keeps it whizzing right along. Consider replacing your current reaction-driven program of copping an attitude with the choice-driven program of adopting an attitude. This new programming enhances your dominion.

So how do you know if you are copping or adopting? Ask yourself, "Based on my values (page 62-63), am I acting/behaving the way I say I want to live? Am I honoring my values with my current attitude?" Even if it is a life-threatening, career-limiting, health-altering, pivotal point, ask yourself those questions. Your values will serve as your inner guidance system. You are totally unique, and your values are your compass, altimeter, speedometer, and global positioning system all rolled into one.

If in the moment, you find that you are better served by reacting rather than by following your values, then you are facing a conflict between your actual values and the set of values you think you hold. Do not be discouraged; this is valuable information. Use this information to reexamine your values and clarify what is true and meaningful to you.

Alternatively, this conflict may reflect you have slipped into some old patterns that you are trying to recondition. This is also valuable information. It helps you understand where you are in the process. Shake it off; literally bounce up and down and shake off the attitude you don't want to have. Reconnect with what you do want for yourself and your life, and then alter your behavior accordingly. You see, it's like we tell our children, "You're a good kid. It's your behavior that I'm not pleased with." You can change your behavior by choice. Choose a different attitude.

As hinted at above, you may wish to adopt different values. You may have inherited some that don't serve you. The great thing is you are not stuck with them. You have total freedom to choose values that do serve you. The key is to make sure you choose what you want for yourself and not what you think you are supposed to choose. Do it for you. Nobody is looking over your shoulder. Nobody is judging you. You aren't competing for the Person with Perfect Values Lifetime Achievement Award.

Remember that you can always change them again as you travel through life learning new things and making new distinctions. That's the fun part of this game. You get to make changes so you can win.

When you are trying on a new attitude, you might feel a little awkward or uncomfortable at first. That's okay if it is an attitude that you have chosen consciously, because it is aligned with your true values. You may not feel totally on track with it yet, but you are practicing. Soon it will feel natural. I know that keeping a positive attitude when things appear to be crumbling down around you is not all that easy, but in the end you'll find that it's better than the alternative. Remember, attitude is just an expression of thought and what follows thought is form. The form will come. Hold that thought!

Take action and move forward in your quest. Be aware of your thoughts, beliefs, and rules. Eliminate the bad thoughts and nurture the good ones that serve you. Check your beliefs; are they accurate or are they outdated? Have you evaluated your rules for the current game, and can you win with them? For example, When you were five, you may have been told don't talk to strangers. Actually, that is a good rule. However, if you are thirty-five and in sales and somewhere in your rule book you still have this rule it can be mighty difficult to engage with prospective clients that you don't know and develop a rapport and relationship with them to convert them to clients. Not that it can't be done. It's just that we have these hidden rules that we are dragging along with us through the years that may not serve us anymore. Take a look at your rule book from time to time and update it. It's your life, your game; you make the rules.

Are you beginning to see how simple it really is to set the game up so you can win? Imagine two filing cabinets in the office space that is your mind: one has the positive files and the other has the negative files. You always have a choice of which cabinet's files you will access for each situation in your life. Simply be aware of which cabinet you are going to open. Be sensitive to how and what you think. You can control your thoughts. Don't let your thoughts control you. This kind of awareness is absolutely crucial to having clarity in your life. If you are constantly choosing content from the negative cabinet, guess what is going to show up in your life?

To make this analogy even more real and effective for you, picture the positive cabinet as one of the most beautiful cabinets you've ever seen. Lock the vision into your mind. Now, imagine the negative cabinet. It's the most hideous, gross, disgusting thing you have ever seen. It's beat up, the drawers stick, there is some kind of slimy ooze on the handles, it smells bad; it's utterly repelling. Make it something that you just really would not even want to get near.

Now that you have your cabinets in place, it's time to clean up the scattered and mixed up files that clutter your mind. There may be a fair number of negative files open on the desk, piles stacked on top of the credenza; it's probably a chore just to find carpet to walk on to get in and out of your mind's office without stepping on the strewn files all over the floor.

Let's identify and sort the strewn files into a positive pile and a negative pile. It is easy to tell them apart, because the positive ones are nice and neat, color-coded with your favorite colors. The negative thought files are torn and falling apart and they smell bad. If there is a color that repulses you, all your negative files are that color.

Put all the positive files into the positive cabinet and all the negative files into the negative cabinet. As you file away those negative thoughts, recognize that they may have served you at one time, but now you don't need them any more. For each negative folder you file away, be sure to create a positive folder. The positive folders will go in the positive cabinet and balance out the negatives. This is easy to do because the positive is usually just the opposite of the negative. For example, if we come across the folder containing "I don't know how to do this," we can create the positive folder containing "This can be done; I just need to learn how." Once you've removed the folders from the floor and organized them into the appropriate cabinet, you'll feel clearer and have more space in your mind to get to the real business of living your best life.

To make the negative cabinet even more real and repulsive, after you have all the negative files identified and filed away, lock up that cabinet and make it extremely difficult to get into. Imagine that the odor from this loathsome cabinet makes you gag. If you stay away from it, you don't smell it. Add this kind of detail to your image of the negative cabinet so that you will want to stay far away from it.

By contrast, make the positive cabinet more real and attractive by experiencing the most inviting smell when you go near it. You love working with it; opening it is a joy. You feel on top of the world knowing this is your cabinet and from it you can easily access the right file every time.

Now look at the floor of your mental office space. Has

removing the clutter revealed a rut that you created by going to either of the cabinets? Which cabinet does the rut lead to? The rut usually leads to the negative, and there is not much difference between a rut and a grave. We are refurbishing this office, so fill in the rut. Give yourself a nice new carpet, and make progress by working with the contents of the positive files.

By reconditioning your mind in this way you will allow yourself to change your mental and emotional environment, which will lead to change much more easily than sheer will-power. Notice your thinking and your behavior going forward after having done this simple exercise. Be aware and appreciate how you are changing.

The hardest part about getting out of a rut is deciding to do so. Why? Because it has become familiar, comfortable, and it is what you know. It has become predictable. Practice controlling the way you think, respond, and react to the stimuli you encounter in the outside world over which you may not have control. This is how you can influence results in the outside world. It's all about experiencing pleasing results.

Chapter 11

Live in HOPE

"Your present circumstances don't determine where you can go; they merely determine where you start."
—NIDO QUBEIN

While wrapping up a coaching session, my client finished with the comment, "I can't be responsible for how my parents treated me when I was child." In essence she was saying it wasn't her fault, but rather it was her parents' fault that she behaved a certain way. As she was saying that, a thought popped into my head, and I blurted out, "If you don't own it you can't discard it." She asked me to repeat it. Until you take ownership of something, either good or bad, it is not yours to throw away. Once you really own your perspective on past events, because that's really all it is—a perspective—you can then change your perspective. The only thing that is real is NOW. The past is only a memory filtered through your current lens.

On the other hand the future has not occurred yet. Whatever, you fantasize it to be is only that—a glorious fantasy or a heinous nightmare. For many it is a daymare they can't snap out of. You can recognize somebody trapped in a daymare. They are the epitome of the worrywart caught in the vortex of the downward spiral of the "What If...." game and careening toward the ground. The choice is yours. Are you trapped in the torturous daydream or hallucinations of guilt (HOG)? Guilt is really nothing more than realizing you made a mistake and reliving it over and over and over. So how do you want to be? How about engaging in hallucinations of positive empowerment (HOPE)? People accustomed to HOG accuse those engaged in HOPE of not being in touch with reality or looking at life through rose-colored glasses. But if NOW is all we really have, and our thoughts are our current reality—so either way it's a hallucination—then why would anyone choose HOG rather than HOPE?

I am reminded of playing Monopoly with my two boys who are eight and four years old. My eight-year-old is a whiz at the game. He understands the rules and the strategies very well. My four-year-old's rules are different. In his version of the game, you roll the dice and move your game piece around the board a number of spaces that doesn't have to be congruent with the number indicated by the dice. Also, he is not required to part from his money when buying property. The eight-year-old accuses the four-year-old of cheating. Calling someone a cheat is pretty harsh. Here's what I tell my eight-year-old . . . pay attention: If you don't know or understand the rules and you make a move that is in violation of those rules then you are not cheating. You can't cheat if you don't know the rules. Now, if I ask my four-year-old, he will tell me that he knows the rules, of course. He thinks he understands the rules and instructions that came in the box with the game because on the surface he is going through the same motions as everybody else. Roll the dice, move the game piece, collect a property card, and so on. However, the rules that he does know, and therefore play by, are his very own. Even though there is no real consequence of the four-year-old playing his game within our game, it drives the 8-year-old nuts. Meanwhile, the four-year-old can't understand why big brother is getting so upset and calling him a cheater. After all, according to his rules he is not cheating; he is playing with HOPE.

Do you have anybody in your life that is, either implicitly or explicitly, accusing you of being a "cheater," "imposter," or "not being responsible," because you are not playing the game based on their rules? List those people here:

____

____

____

Don't live a HOG lifestyle. Realize that we each have a game and our own set of rules. Do your rules still apply or do you need to update them? Be honest with yourself, and then play by your rules.

List the rules you want to examine: ____________________

____

____

____

____

____

On the flip side, who in your life is not playing by your rules and is consequently driving you nutso?
List them here: ______________________________

____

____

____

____

Go back to the scene of the Monopoly game; are you being the eight-year-old getting mad at the four-year-old who is playing by a different set of rules? Are you thinking, "But they should know the rules!"? If so, that thought may spring from one of your rules that may be keeping you from winning. When you catch those "shoulds," "woulds," and "coulds" creeping into your thoughts, consider reevaluating how you have set up your rules. As you know, life did not come to us with a set of rules or instructions. We get to make it up as we go. So live in HOPE and not HOG! That's a fundamental rule for winning!

The transition from HOG to HOPE is another exercise in changing perspective. If you can change your perspective, you can change your life. What follows are eight specific and basic steps to making that transformation.

1. Identify and label the current situation or area of difficulty. Can you name how you feel about your situation? For example, you may feel stuck, cornered, off-track, bummed, or overwhelmed. Identify and name what it is for you. You may not even recognize it. However, if you are saying things like "It's just a fact of life," "That's just the way it is," and "It's out of my control," then you are probably experiencing a situation or area of your life in which you are stuck. This, of course, is only a single, less-than-positive point of view. In fact, what you are experiencing is your current perspective on how life is. It is where you are coming from. This is what happens when you are not in the driver's seat of your own life.

Let's take exercise for example, or lack of exercise as the case may be. You might be saying to yourself, "there just isn't enough time to fit in a workout with my schedule." So your current perspective is "No time." You must realize that this is only one angle for viewing the given situation. You may have become so entrenched in this point of view that you are not aware of any others. You may be stuck in this particular rut, and the view from here sucks! If it were really the case of not having enough time, then how is it that others with a schedule twice or even five times as full as yours can squeeze in some exercise every other day? Do you imagine for a moment that someone like Madonna has a schedule less hectic than yours. She finds time to work out. The same is true for the President of the United States, top CEOs, and soccer moms. What do you think their perspective might be regarding exercising?

We all have the same 960 waking minutes each day, assuming you don't sleep more than eight hours a night. The only difference is in how we decide to use those minutes. If you work out for forty-five minutes and allow another forty minutes for travel and shower that is still less than 9% of your waking day. 540 minutes go into a nine-hour workday. That leaves 420 minutes to do what you really want to do. By these calculations, the eighty-five minutes you need to work out will take up 20% of your available 420 minutes of free time. You still need to pick up the kids, cook dinner, spend time with the family, tuck the kids into bed, put some time in on the special project, take time to pay the bills, journal, and script…the list goes on and on.

Remember, the part where I said, "to do what you really want to do"? I didn't say what you "should do" or "could do." Remember the twelve-foot pole, the want? Until you collapse the want, the object of the want will elude you. Pull these together. Identify what you want, then experience it now. It is your perspective that stands in your way. Instead of wanting to exercise every other day, remove the want; exercise every other day. Proportion your time to make it happen. Employ the perspective that you do have the time and you can exercise every other day.

To aid you in making the identification, questions such as, "Why must I have X?", "Why do I have X?", or "Why is having X important to me?" are more useful than a question such as, "Why do I want X?" You get drastically different answers and results. The answers to the "have" questions will bring you to what is already yours. The answer to the "want" questions will keep you from it. It's as simple as flipping the magnet.

Have you noticed how two magnets can actually repel each other when both the positive ends are put together or both the negative ends are put together. Furthermore, if you turn one of the magnets around they join instantly. Apply this physics to your life. Remember that thoughts are simply a vibration; a vibrational energy that resonates and attracts its same vibrational energy Do you have the right thought or perspective—the attractive side of the magnet—facing what is yours? Or is the repellant side facing what is yours? Do you have too many things between you and what is yours, diluting the power of your thought and separating you from what is yours?

So, step one is simply giving your current perspective on life a label. By asking yourself, "How am I choosing to look at this current situation? Where am I coming from?" you will identify and name your perspective.

2. Identify other possible perspectives. Ask yourself, "What's another way to look at the situation? How would I like to be able to look at it? Where would I like to be coming from?"

If you've identified the current repelling side of the magnet as "stuck," "disempowered," or "why bother," for example, what would the name of the attractive side be? ____________________

____

Good. What would another attractive side be? ______________

____

Excellent! Get as many as these of you can. List at least 7 attractive alternatives.

____

____

____

____

____

____

____

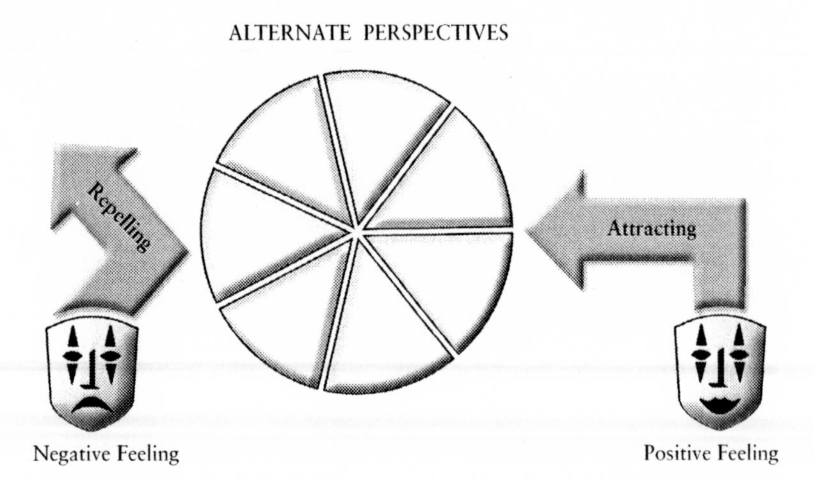

Transfer the seven alternate perspectives to the sections of the magnet in the diagram above. Now determine if your current perspective is what is facing or pointing towards the object, situation, or experience you must have. Is your perspective repelling or attracting? Label the repelling or the attracting arrow with your current perspective. Of your seven alternative perspectives, choose the most attractive one and align it with your object.

3. Try them on. You have identified where you are coming from. You have come up with several other perspectives for how you would like to be approaching your situation. Now it is time to step into each of these possible perspectives and determine which will serve you best. Remember that you can always go back to what you started with. I am not here to take anything away from you. I am here to help broaden your horizons, provoke you to discover what's really inside of you, and play big! Are you ready?

Choose the perspective that you think and feel would achieve your havingness. Really get into it. Get up if you are sitting, and move to another place in the room. This will change your immediate, physical perspective and support the change in your mental perspective. Picture in front of you a wedge the shape of this new perspective you are going to embrace. When you are ready take in a big breath and embrace this new perspective. Imagine what it is like living from this perspective. Breathe as if you are the essence of your chosen new perspective and feel how different this new perspective feels. Use your imagination and stand as if you know in your bones you have achieved. Move as if; really feel as if. Picture the situation as if. How do you feel about the situation now? Good! Excellent!

Okay...shake it out. Let go of that perspective and try on one of the other perspectives you came up with. Not later. Right now! Come on... When you are ready, take in a big NEW (Now Empowering Wisdom) breath, and embrace this new perspective. Imagine what it is like living from this perspective. Breathe as if you are the essence of your chosen new perspective and feel how different this new perspective feels. Use your imagination and stand as if you know in your bones you have achieved. Move as if; really feel as if. Picture the situation as if. How do you feel about the situation now? Awesome!

Let's do one more.... Shake it out. When you are ready consume a big new breath and embrace this new perspective. Imagine what it is like living from this perspective. Breathe as if you are the essence of your chosen new perspective and feel how different this new perspective feels. Use your imagination and stand as if you know in your bones you have achieved. Move as if; really feel as if. Picture the situation as if. How do you feel about the situation now? Great!

I am proud of you for going for it on this one. You'll be glad you did. If you feel you need to try on some other perspectives, go for it! If you feel you have found one that works for you, then we can move on.

4. Choose the perspective you feel serves you best. Shake everything out. Once again, embrace the perspective that you have chosen for yourself. When you are ready consume a big new breath and embrace this new perspective. Imagine what it is like living from this perspective. Breathe as if you are the essence of your chosen new perspective and feel how different this new perspective feels. Use your imagination and stand as if you know in your bones you have achieved. Move as if; really feel as if. Picture the situation as if. How do you feel about the situation now? Now double that feeling. Good! Now magnify it by ten! Spend a little extra time picturing the situation from this perspective. Remember you are an all powerful attractive magnet for what is yours. In your mind, line yourself up on target. You may even want to physically redirect where you are facing. Imagine all obstacles out of your way; see a direct and clear path between you and your having what is already yours. It is available to you to be had. Now, by practicing this perspective, you are making yourself available to it! Only three more steps....stay with me.

5. Create a plan that addresses the situation. From your new perspective begin with the end in mind. See yourself having what is already yours. Know you achieved this through living and being in this perspective. Now that you have it, work backwards. What are the thoughts you must think? What are the actions you must do? Why did you think those thoughts and do those things? Take the answers, and script your plan.

Remember a good plan today is far better than a best plan tomorrow. Do this now! Write something down now! The power is in the now!

6. Commit to the plan and to yourself. Keep reminding yourself, this is your game and you make the rules. This can be easy or hard. You decide. You do have to commit, though. There is a difference between being interested and being committed. When you are interested, you do what you must do when it is convenient for you. When you are committed, you do what you must do when it must be done. There is no time better than right now. You are either committed to having or you aren't. Which is it? There is no in between. Hurl yourself at that which you desire and the universe will bring it to you.

Be aware you may have to say "No" to some things in order to achieve, and you may need to say "Yes" to certain things as well. Let's go back to our scenario of fitting in time to work out. As we discussed, there are only so many minutes in the day. Nobody is an alchemist when it comes to time. We all get the same dose. Therefore, if something is important to have, we may need to take something out so as to make room. Perhaps you need to say "No" to lying on the couch for 2 hours each night to unwind. Maybe it's "No" to hitting the snooze the 2nd, 3rd, or 4th time. It could be "No" to going to lunch with the gang at work. Come up with two or three things that you must say "No" to in order to have what you must have. And come up with two or three things you must say "Yes" to. Maybe it is "Yes" to getting up an hour earlier to accommodate the workout. It might be "Yes" to getting yourself a personal trainer if this provides you the motivation, discipline, and accountability you need. It could be saying "Yes" to joining a gym or buying some exercise equipment. Determine what it is for you, and say "yes!"

Now add to your plan the things you are willing to say "no" to and the things you are willing to say "yes" to.

In order to be me, I am willing to say NO to the following:

____

____

____

____

____

And I am willing to say YES to the following:

____

____

____

____

____

Are you willing to commit to do what it takes to have what is yours in your life? Since the answer is a resounding "yes," I want you to picture a line on the ground. You can make it with a piece of tape or you can find a seam or pattern in the carpet. We have come a long way in expanding the list of options, choosing a perspective, and creating a plan. Now there's the line on the floor. Take a deep new breath when you are ready to commit to the plan and say "yes!" to the key elements and "no!" to the distractions. Now, when you are truly ready to commit to this new way of being, step across the line.

Once you cross the line you will notice a shift in your being. This is powerful. Let's keep the momentum going.

7. Take action. This should feel easy compared to all the work and commitment you just accomplished. From your list, select one item and start. If one of your items was to join a gym, then make some calls and schedule an orientation for yourself. The action can be as simple as setting a new time on your alarm clock. Chances are you are so pumped up at the shift within you that you want to do a lot. That's great! Go for it! Do something, anything to forward the action.

Will this empowering title wave of emotion last forever? Most likely not. Might you slip off track in a week or two? Perhaps. When you feel the empowering emotion fading, remember to find your perspective and fully connect with it all over again as you did in Step 4. Set your environment. Play your favorite music; smell your favorite scents. If you love the outdoors, be there. While in your best possible environment, review your action plan for a couple minutes each day while fully connecting with it. Put yourself in the picture. Be in the picture. This will help you to stay on track. As long as you are honoring your values while you build your plan and take action on your plan, you are assured success.

8. Be accountable. Commit to a coach or a buddy that you will do certain key actions within your plan by a certain date. We may break a commitment to ourselves, but we usually won't break the commitment with others so easily. Here is an example of how accountability works. Let's say you commit to walking for forty minutes every other day at 6:30 a.m. You do it the first couple of times, and then there is that one morning where the warm sheets feel too good. Rather than rolling out of bed, you want to roll over in bed. You rationalize that it's only one day, and it's no big deal. And then one day turns into one week, and then one month, and finally you are no better off than when you started. Alternatively, having decided to be accountable, you find a friend or colleague who also wants to walk, and you commit to walking with them on a regular schedule. Now when the alarm rings you get up and go because you don't want to let Bill down. Maybe you even made a side bet with Bill that the first one to not show up for the walk owes the other one $500. Are you getting it? Find and create a structure that works to motivate or even trick you into doing what you ultimately must to do to get the end results that are yours for the having.

In a nutshell the eight steps to adopting a new perspective are:

1. Identify your current perspective.
2. Identify other possible perspectives.
3. Try them on.
4. Choose a new perspective.
5. Create a plan to employ your new perspective.
6. Commit to the plan and to yourself.
7. Take action.
8. Be accountable.

If you find yourself slipping into a funk, copping an attitude about your NEW perspectives and plan of action, turn on some music. Get your body moving. Recount some of your blessings. This will banish the invisible pressure and pretty soon you may even forget what you were bummed about. This works great for the day-to-day issues that we allow in to fog our day.

It is important to note that there are seasons in life. Sometimes there are moments to feel sad, defeated, or hurt. Don't try to avoid or make quick-fixes when the emotions are important and appropriate. Much personal learning can come from experiencing the entire spectrum of emotions. Give yourself time. Understand the difference between bad attitudes and perspectives versus appropriate expression of emotions. If you find it hard to really tell the difference, there are many books and professionals that can assist you in learning the distinction. Don't be afraid to get yourself the resources and help you need to live your best life.

Chapter 12

Choose to Change

"Watch your thoughts; they become words.
Watch your words; they become actions.
Watch your actions; they become habits.
Watch your habits; they become character.
Watch your character; it becomes your destiny."
— PATRICK OVERTON

In order to survive happily, you must become a good change agent. Life is overflowing with change. There is always going to be more to do than you can do. Establish the rules that permit you to win at the change game known as life. For me, just the realization that life is a game of mastering change was a big help. That one understanding and distinction has allowed me to blast through a lot of anger. Once you get it, problems seem to dissolve. It's questionable if they were really there. From one perspective there was most certainly a problem, and yet from another perspective there was none. A wonderful resource for learning to deal with change is Dr. Spencer Johnson's book *Who Moved My Cheese?*

Here is how simple it really all is. Each of us is born knowing "It." We just have to trust that we know the answers for ourselves. Furthermore, we spend the rest of our lives trying to remember what "It" is and learning to grant ourselves permission to trust that we do know the answers. All is available to us as we need it. If, from what you have read in this book so far, you can begin to understand these truths, I have succeeded.

Consider the fact that a baby is born with only two fears—the fear of falling and the fear of loud noises. All the other fears we learn while we are in the world. Fear is the absence of love. When I see the phrase "NO FEAR," I think pure love. So we are born with only two fears and the rest of our constitution is a bursting bundle of pure love.

Then it begins. We start learning the many forms of fear and prejudice. The fear of not being good enough, the fear of failure, fear of success, fear of rejection, fear of not doing it right, fear of getting hurt either physically or emotionally, fear of you-name-it. So, what most of us do as we go through life is, in essence, unlearn or forget the wisdom that we came into the world with—that we are most free and happy when love is all we know. We then become a mass of immobilized unhappy scaredy-cats. Or worse yet, we do things to ourselves and others out of reactionary fear. You can quote me on this one: "Fear is the root of all evil."

Insecurity—the biggest bundle of fear—is why people hurt other people verbally, emotionally, and physically. Think about it. If you are confident that you are complete and whole in all that you are and all that you do, and if you know that nobody can threaten you in any way, would you feel you have to threaten or hurt them? Of course not. A healthy adult does not have the inclination to harm a baby. Why? A baby is the closest thing to pure love. It brings no real threats. But if someone at work is trying for the same promotion you are and their strategy to "win" is to make you look bad, you may experience fear. If your girlfriend or spouse looks at another guy with interest, you experience the fear that she may leave. The fear you feel in both of these examples might lead you to do or say things that are hurtful to the others involved. This is your reaction to your feelings of fear. On the other hand, if you are the most attractive person to your girlfriend and you treat her with only love and respect, you really seek to understand her, making her feel totally loved by you, can you imagine her ever wanting to leave? I don't think so. Treat people the way they want to be treated and the fear will melt away—both theirs and yours. A great start to purging much of your fear is to stop watching the news. Believe me if something is that important for you to be aware of you will learn of it in time to prepare for whatever it is. If your business or profession depends on being current on the days events then calibrate wisely. This is really about controlling the information that you are exposed to and how you react to it. Most people are familiar with the phrase garbage in garbage out. I would go as far to say that it is garbage in garbage in. When it comes to all of the negative messages that we are continuously exposed to via the television, newspapers, movies and other forms of media we become unwarily conditioned of those messages. Be cognizant and monitor and control what comes into your world, your mind and your being.

So, think about the baby for a second. Babies actually welcome change and change is good, especially when it comes to diapers. So the moral of this chapter is be a baby and welcome change in a spirit of pure love. Grow up and be a master change agent. Love evolves Love.

In Conclusion

Are you still wondering what the purpose of your life is and why you are here? This is a huge question. It should not be taken lightly.

I don't think I was alone when I searched and searched and searched for the meaning. Why am I here? What is the purpose of my life? I would ponder these questions and wait for some flash of brilliance to consume me. I would wait for the heavens to part and the message to come down to me from the sun beams. I would wait for the all powerful voice to vibrate my bones with my mission.

In the science of physics it is accepted that if you change the way you look at things, the things you look at will change. We are right back to perspectives. You have a choice from which perspective you view yourself and the world around you. Albert Einstein said that perhaps the most important decision you can make is whether you view the world as a hostile environment or a friendly environment. Make excellent use of your free will.

By changing the way I looked at things what I finally realized was that every day for years and years I was trading the present for the future. I was letting life slip away. I was sitting on the side lines waiting for the game to start and not realizing it was well into the second quarter. Have you ever heard the term "getting ready to get ready"? Well I was the poster child for that one. Then the other day I heard it, loud and clear. Not from the heavens. Angelic music did not burst out. The clouds did not form the message. The thunderous voice did not consume my being and instill the message. Well at least not the way you might think. It came to me through conversation with my coach, while working on this book. This is huge!

Remember I just mentioned that I was the poster child for "getting ready to get ready"? Well, there was a time when I thought I would have to have this whole book finished before I started tickling the key board and actually write it. My goal in this book is to share a little wisdom with you, wisdom that I gained through years and years of experience, to help you with some answers to your questions. However, I discovered a key message of wisdom at well over 25,000 words into this book. And if I can get this then I have no doubt you can too. The flash is this. The purpose of your life is... what you make it; it is whatever you decide it is! No matter what your answer is, you are right! And it can certainly change as you grow and learn throughout your life.

For me this is a huge breakthrough—a catapult out of frustration into wisdom. I was waiting to get it perfect, to know that once I was on the track, it was the right track, and I wouldn't have to turn back. Only then could I confidently advance with total conviction down that "right" path. And I was thinking that the message, mission, quest, purpose—whatever you call it—would be somehow injected into me and fill my being. So far it hasn't happened that way, and I choose not to wait any longer. I just assumed that all the people I thought had their life together and seemed on purpose had some secret that I was not blessed with yet. And then—BOOM— I got it. If it is meant to be then it is up to me...determining my purpose that is. For me, at this time in my life, my purpose is to provoke brilliance in others as well as in myself. That's why I am writing this book and coaching people. I believe that inside every one of us is an abundance of brilliance. I have learned some tricks and strategies to help people get reacquainted with their brilliance and reengage with their magnificence.

I love the truth that the purpose of life is what you make it. First, it is a discovery process. It may not always feel like or be an epiphany. It may take some time for you to decide what it should be or to allow yourself to let it be what you want. It can also happen in an instant, which it did for me in the course of a conversation. Second, it comes from within rather than from outside. When you know and you know you know, confidence replaces fear. There is a saying that I have adopted as a core belief for me: Prayer or meditation is talking to God. Intuition is God talking to us. Follow your gut. Learn to trust your inner wisdom, which is God. When you trust yourself you are trusting in the same wisdom that created you.

Let me tell you the story of the man who lost his keys. He was searching frantically for his keys outside in the driveway. These keys were to his treasured possessions, his home, his car, his business, and such. A neighbor came upon him and asked if he could help with the search. The man replied, "Yes, I've lost my keys. Can you help me find them?" They both searched for about a half hour with no luck. The neighbor asked, "Are you sure you lost your keys out here?" The man replied, "No, I think I lost them in the den but the light is better out here."

Are you searching in the right place? I know I wasn't. I was looking outside. "Show me the signs. Show me the way!" was my mantra. It was a pretty whiney one too. I assumed the light was out there somewhere. The signs and the way were not showing up as I expected them out there. Rather, they were on the inside in the forms of inklings, intuition, thoughts, and feelings. It took a lot of discipline for me to quiet my mind and look inside. Looking inside of yourself and honoring your thoughts, inklings, intuition, feelings, and visions is the map to your life's treasures.

What are you ignoring in your life right now? What is the crazy, hectic noise of day-to-day living covering up that you need to be hearing? What is getting in the way of your vision of who you really are in this world? What have you allowed to numb your senses?

Think of it for the last time. Be free of the self-imposed limitations. Focus on what is your divine birth right and start living today. Start really living your life your way!

Going on the inside allows us to happily achieve rather than going on the outside flailing to achieve happiness.

Keep in mind this is a philosophy and not a science. Philosophy is asking questions that don't have answers. Once you prove the answer it becomes science. I would love to tell you that I have it all figured out, and that this is the science of how life works. However, it is the amalgamation of my thoughts and questions that make up my philosophy.

My mission was to have provoked your brilliance. If reading this book has inspired a new thought for you or redirected your thinking down a more empowering path, then I am on purpose and you are on your way too. Thank your for your time, attention, and focus. It is dear to me. We may not have actually met face-to-face; however our spirits have touched through these words. I would love to hear and read about your journey of growth. Write me, call me, or come up to me at a seminar, and be sure to let me know how you are doing on your journey. What's next for you and your wildly successful and enjoyable life?

Machen MacDonald delivers the powerful strategies
and techniques
detailed in *Provoking Your Brilliance!*
to companies and individuals.

Other presentations include:

- ***Setting and Achieving Your Brilliant Goals***
- ***Brilliantly Adapting to Change***
- ***Getting Brilliant Customers Fast***
- ***Brilliantly Managing Yourself in Relation To Time***

For more information on speaking, coaching, seminars and workshops, contact Machen at:

12114 Polaris Drive, Grass Valley, CA 95949
Tel. (530) 273-8000 — eFax (530) 687-8583
www.ProBrilliance.com

Want to order copies of this book for employees,
colleagues, friends or family?
Contact Machen as above or use the order forms
on the following pages.

ORDER FORM

Item	Description	Quantity	Unit	Total
#001	Provoking Your Brilliance!		$17.95/ea.	________
	Tax (CA residents add 8.25%)		$1.48/ea.	________
	Shipping and Handling within the continental U.S.			$4.95/ea
			TOTAL	________

Method of Payment:

☐ Check Enclosed (payable to ProBrilliance!)

☐ MasterCard ☐ Visa ☐ American Express ☐ Discover

Billing Address:

Please print. To ensure successful processing of your order, please be sure that the billing address you enter matches the billing address of the credit card you are using.

Name as It Appears on Card: ____________________

Street Address: ____________________

City: ____________________ State: ____________

Country (if outside U.S.) ____________________ Postal Code: ____________

Credit Card #: ____________________

Exp. Date. ____________________ Sec. Code ____________

Shipping Address if different from above: ____________________

____

The undersigned purchaser certifies that he or she has read and understands all of the terms and conditions on this invoice. All the terms and conditions are part of this sales order, which shall constitute a contract between parties, and there are no expressed or implied warranties, modifications, or performance guarantees other than expressly stated herein.

Cardholder's Signature ____________________

Date ____________________

Please fax your completed form to
(530) 687-8583 or mail with payment to

ProBrilliance!
12114 Polaris Drive, Grass Valley, CA 95949
Telephone: (530) 273-8000
E-Mail: CoachMach@yahoo.com www.ProBrilliance.com

Printed in the United States
26219LVS00002B/91-510